INDIA'S NATIONAL SECURITY CHALLENGES

INDIA'S NATIONAL
SECURITY CHALLENGES

edited by
N.N. VOHRA

INDIA
INTERNATIONAL
CENTRE

PRIMUS
BOOKS

PRIMUS BOOKS

An Imprint of Ratna Sagar P. Ltd.
Virat Bhavan
Mukherjee Nagar Commercial Complex
Delhi 110 009

Offices at
CHENNAI   LUCKNOW
AGRA AHMEDABAD BANGALORE COIMBATORE
DEHRADUN GUWAHATI HYDERABAD JAIPUR JALANDHAR
KANPUR KOCHI KOLKATA MADURAI MUMBAI
PATNA RANCHI VARANASI

First Published 2023

ISBN: 978-93-5852-037-8 (hardback)
ISBN: 978-93-5852-038-5 (PoD)

Published by Primus Books

Contents

Preface

One of the objectives of the India International Centre, New Delhi (IIC) is to foster meaningful debates on the existing and arising challenges confronting us and the world. Among the many problems facing India, the IIC has been organising a continuing series of talks and discussions on various aspects of national security.

In early 2021, when the COVID-19 pandemic was once again rearing its head, it was not possible to organize programmes involving the physical presence of participants. It was, therefore, decided to hold a series of on-line discussions, popularly referred to as 'webinars', on issues concerning national security.

Deviating from the earlier pattern of largely inviting academics and strategic analysts to speak on homeland and external security related problems, we decided that this time around we would listen to the views of former practitioners, retired veterans of the three Defence Services and, besides, of a few commentators. For the benefit of all those who have serious interest in national security affairs, we also decided to bring out a volume containing the views expressed in the debates organised at the IIC.

Any discussion on safeguarding the country's security involves reflection on a host of issues. We decided to focus on the following aspects:

- the Union Government's policy for safeguarding national security and the responsibilities of the Union and the States in respect thereof;
- issues relating to defence management and the need for systemic reforms.

The pages following reflect the opinions of known veterans and, besides, a valuable summarisation of the seminar in which all of them debated issues among themselves.

I am grateful to Admiral (Retd.) Arun Prakash, Air Chief Marshal (Retd.) Fali H. Major, Lt. Gen. (Retd.) D.S. Hooda, Lt. Gen. (Retd.) Philip Campose, Lt. Gen. (Retd.) Satish Dua, Air Vice Marshal (Retd.) Arjun Subramanian, Dr. Ajai Sahni, Cmde (Retd.) C. Uday Bhaskar, and Amb. (Retd.) Sujan R. Chinoy for finding time to participate in the discussions organised at the IIC.

Shortly before he lost his life in a tragic air accident, Bipin Rawat, Chief of Defence Staff, accepted my request to speak at the IIC on the reforms in the Defence sector, which he was then engaged in carrying out. I pay tribute to his memory and the valuable contributions made by this eminent soldier.

I thank IIC Director K.N. Shrivastava, Chief Editor Omita and Chief Programme Division Teteii for their strong support, which has enabled the publication of this volume.

N.N. VOHRA
LIFE TRUSTEE
July 2023
New Delhi
INDIA INTERNATIONAL CENTRE

I

Pressing Need for a National Security Policy

N.N. Vohra

The Constitution of India provides that it shall be the duty of the Union government to protect every State against internal disturbance and external aggression and the States shall be responsible for maintaining police forces and ensuring public order. The Union government is empowered to deploy its armed forces in any part of the country, as per requirement.

Flowing from the aforesaid prescriptions, the Union Ministry of Defence (MoD) is responsible for maintaining external security and guarding the country against war or any threat from across its frontiers, and the Ministry of Home Affairs (MHA) is responsible for the maintenance of internal security and taking all necessary steps to ensure peace and normalcy in the country. Further, as and when need arises, the MHA may deploy contingents of the Central Armed Police Forces (CAPF) in any State for assisting it to restore order in the disturbed area. In certain situations units of the Army may also be inducted, in aid of the civil authority, to contain a serious disturbance. Over the past decades, the

MoD and MHA have been working sectorally, largely on the basis that there are no points of intersection in the discharge of their respective duties.

A fleeting look back on the period since Independence would show that the country has faced a host of continuing internal security problems, among which mention maybe made of the prolonged insurgencies in the Northeast region, some of which began before 1947 and are still active; the unabated violent activities of the Naxal groups (the Leftwing extremists); the Pakistan supported pro-Khalistan disturbances in the Panjab, pre- and post-Operation Blue Star (June 1984); Pakistan's unabated proxy war in Kashmir, which began around end of 1989; and the Pakistani radical networks which perpetually strive to perpetrate sabotage, subversion and terror activities in India.

Considering the scope of this writing, it is not feasible to comment chronologically on the disturbances in the past years or to dilate on the recurring loss of lives and the enormous economic and other damages which have been suffered, time and again, on account of the failures of the States to timely tackle law and order disturbances within their territories. Whatever may have been the circumstances, the MHA has been consistently deploying CAPF contingents for the restoration of normalcy in the affected States. In situations where such deployments were unable to achieve the envisaged results, the Union government has also been deploying the Army, as was done to deal with the disorders in the Northeast region, Panjab and in Jammu and Kashmir. In this context, it would be relevant to recall that after the Army's Operation Blue Star , it took over a decade to contain the situation in Panjab; the Army still remains deployed in the Northeast and continues to be heavily committed in J&K. In this context, for formulating a pragmatic policy for effective internal security management, it would be beneficial to bear in mind that while the Union government may never have defaulted in providing the required assistance for restoring normalcy in any disturbed area, it has been doing so without ever questioning the States about the latter's failure to reform and upgrade the functioning of their police organisations so that they become capable of handling arising situations on their own. This syndrome has also led to the States not being held accountable for their failure to timely take the required politico–administrative initiatives for tackling brewing problems which later enlarged into major disorders.

The aforementioned approach has, regrettably, strengthened the States' convenient belief that the responsibility for maintaining internal order in the country rests more with the Union government than on them.

One of the continuing reasons for the failure of the States to progressively build the requisite capability for tackling internal disorders on their own emanates from the procrastination of successive Union governments to evolve and make known a holistic National Security Policy (NSP) which:

- identifies the objectives of national security and reflects their inter-linkages;
- provides a pragmatic framework within which all the national security organisations/agencies shall operate and be held accountable;
- ensures that the allocations for defence conform to and meet the demands of a known security policy;
- reflects the respective responsibilities of the Union and the States with regard to internal security management.

The NSP would also bring out India's national and international interests, the security threats facing the country from within and without, and the contours of the foreign, defence and homeland policies within which the Union and State governments would need to work together for the maintenance of pan India security, which is imperative for the uninterrupted growth and development of the country and its people.

The lack of an NSP—which would be periodically renewed and re-oriented on the basis of the experiences gained—and the consequential absence of internal security and military doctrines which would flow therefrom, has engendered an environment in which decisions regarding national security continue to be taken on an ad-hoc basis, particularly at times when the country is faced with a crisis situation.

Looking back to the period since the early 1980s: there has been a progressive increase in threats to internal security, both from within the country and from external sources. However, the capability of the State police organizations has not been enhanced to match the increasing challenges. On the contrary, the constabularies are continuing to suffer very large deficiencies because of the apathy of the State governments and poor budgetary support from year to year. Consequently, there has been a failure in increasing the strength of the civil and armed police forces; modernizing their weapons, equipments, communications, transport, investigation, and forensic testing systems and separating the functioning of their prosecution wings. The working of the police has also been adversely affected by political interference and unlawful pressures, which have resulted in fracturing the command and control systems and generating indiscipline, unaccountability and corruption among the ranks. The State governments have also failed to progressively enlarge and improve the resources and capabilities of their intelligence organizations.

It is a matter of grave concern that our justice delivery system also continues to be in a deplorable condition, marred by prolonged delays, inefficiency and corruption. Over 50 million cases have been awaiting trials for prolonged periods in courts all over the country, including hundreds of thousands in the higher courts. Time-bound steps require to be taken to improve the functioning of the judicial system, particularly focusing on the competence and integrity of the subordinate courts.

Law and order cannot be effectively enforced unless the entire justice system functions with speed, efficiency and fairness to ensure prompt completion of investigations, time-bound trials and exemplary punishments to all those found guilty of criminal offences. The MHA must not lose any further time in compelling the States to implement the now very long-pending police reforms. It should also notify the States about the conditions which shall require to be met whenever they seek its help for internal security management. The States could even be asked to bear the costs, partly or fully, of the assistance provided to them and such revenues could be utilized by the MHA for promoting the upgradation of the State police organizations.

While threats to the maintenance of internal security, across the country, have been progressively increasing, there has been inadequate enhancement in the resources and capacities to be prepared for taking on the arising challenges. Today, an unknown adversary, located thousands of miles away, can launch a terror/cyberattack on a target of its choosing and cause untold havoc. Needless to stress, the MHA and its agencies need to be fully trained and equipped to be able to pre-empt such attacks and to be able to respond within seconds to assaults from artificial intelligence, robotic and unarmed systems. To achieve such capability the MHA, which has continued to remain heavily overburdened with varied tasks, would need to be: (i) relieved of all its non-security related responsibilities; (ii) manned by adequately trained personnel who are deployed on at least 10–15 year tenures, if not on a permanent basis; and (iii) the Home Secretary must have a much longer tenure than he presently enjoys. The re-organized MHA, and with all its agencies equipped with the latest technologies and systems, could perhaps be renamed as the Ministry of Internal Security Affairs (MISA). Until the much required changes are brought about, the MHA would benefit by critically reviewing its own functioning, with particular focus on the following areas:

(i) The central Intelligence Bureau (IB) needs to be enlarged, its capabilities technologically strengthened and, side by side, its functioning needs to be monitored to ensure the relevance, promptitude and veracity of its reports and the reliability of its assessments. Besides, a credible oversight mechanism requires to be set up to dynamically overview its functioning: it is of crucial importance to safeguard the integrity of this institution and to effectively ensure against the politicization of its functioning.

(ii) The overall strength of the MHA's armed forces, the CAPF, has increased over the years. There are four border guarding forces: Border Security Force (BSF), Indo-Tibetan Border Police (ITBP), Sashastra Seema Bal and the Assam Rifles, and three which are essentially concerned with internal security management: Central Reserve Police Force (CRPF), Central Industrial

Security Force (CISF) and the National Security Guard (NSG). However, as has been repeatedly happening, for meeting emergent situations, the MHA has been, time and again, pulling out the border guarding forces and deploying them on internal security duties, for which they were never trained and equipped. The benefit of having several forces, with different names, to perform the same role, could be beneficially reviewed. There is also urgent need to critically re-assess the required force levels of the CAPF. This exercise would need to be done within a rolling perspective plan of say 5–7 years and, thereafter, every Force should be enabled to timely achieve its increased strength so that each CAPF becomes adequately equipped and capable of meeting its responsibilities and there is no future occasion for the border guarding forces to be withdrawn from the frontiers. Furthermore, as the nature of threats on both the external and internal fronts become growingly complex, it is imperative that the CAPF meant for internal security management and border guarding are made to undergo periodic refresher and re-orientation training courses so that they fully understand the nature of the upcoming challenges and the manner in which they would require to be handled. It is also essential that all the CAPF are equipped with the best arms, and the latest technology equipments and systems, which would fully meet their operational requirements.

(iii) For the lack of an internal security policy, the Army has been recurringly involved in dealing with internal disorders. This is not a pleasing reflection on the MHA's functioning. If the essential reason for involving the Army in the management of internal security duties is to secure additional troops which are better trained and equipped as compared to the CAPF, then there is no reason whatsoever why the MHA cannot upgrade its own armed forces or raise a new force which is as well trained, equipped and trustworthy as the Army's infantry. However, it is not known whether the MHA has ever made a demand for raising a new internal security force, trained and equipped to the highest professional standards, which can adequately handle the varied challenges on the internal security front.[1]

One way or another, there cannot be any debate that the Army must not be routinely involved in internal security management. This important matter merits being urgently reviewed by the Union government and a clear decision taken to entrust the entire responsibility of internal security management to the MHA, the Army being involved only in very exceptional situations which have external security ramifications. Such a decision will not only ease the existing pressure on the Army's infantry force levels but also protect it from severe criticism, frequently voiced, that the soldiers on internal security duties violate the human rights of local populations.[2] It would also be beneficial to ensure that, whenever the Army is to be involved, the formal decision in the matter is preceded by a clear listing of the tasks to be performed by it, the goals to be achieved and the envisaged timeframe for the withdrawal of the Army's units. It must be remembered that large scale and prolonged deployment of Army units for carrying out internal security/counter-insurgency duties is extremely damaging: besides exhausting the troops it adversely impacts their essential training and engenders a psychology which is detrimental to their primary role of safeguarding the country's frontiers.

(iv) The MHA should set up an internal cell, comprising experienced practitioners, to revisit every case in which the CAPF and the Army had to be deployed in the States (say, within the last 10–15 years) and to critically examine the root causes of the internal disturbances which necessitated such deployments. The findings of the aforesaid research and analysis would be of crucial importance for rebuilding the architecture of internal security management on a pragmatic basis.

It would be found that in a large majority of the cases the State police has invariably failed to timely deal with the initial occurrence which, with the passage of time and the free interplay of partisan political interests, has evolved into a major disturbance.[3] In this context, the MHA would do well to issue a binding directive to all States to ensure that, besides dealing with the law and order aspect of any disturbance, they must devote special attention to also deal with the root causes which triggered the initial disorder.

Another matter for concern: as past experience has shown, whenever there are incipient reports of trouble brewing from the conflict of partisan interests, hostile foreign agencies, which are perpetually on the prowl, speedily jump into the fray to trigger large scale disturbances. It is important that the Central and State intelligence agencies exercise unceasing vigil on every front and keep all concerned authorities timely alerted.

In the past years, Pakistan has been displaying increasing belligerence: cross border infiltration and terrorist attacks in J&K have been stepped up and continuing attempts are being made to smuggle large quantities of drugs, munitions and fake Indian currency across the Line of Control (LOC) via drone droppings. Side by side, for the past several years now, the Chinese military has also been triggering serious confrontations along and across the Line of Actual Control (LAC), which could, at any time, enlarge into full scale military conflicts. This situation has, understandably, compelled the Indian defence forces, particularly the Army, to mobilize on both the Pakistan and China fronts to counter any arising eventuality.

Besides being a matter for serious concern, the now long continuing situation along the LAC has also highlighted the need for very large investments which would require to be made for adequately strengthening our defence lines and undertaking the much needed development of the border areas. Needless to say, all this would require to be done on the basis of a well-conceived strategy. Meanwhile, it would be fruitful to secure maximum possible optimization of the available military resources and to particularly ensure that the present strength of the Army's infantry is not frittered away in deployments in aid of the civil authority. As an immediate solution: groups of neighbouring States and Union Territories—say, J&K, Ladakh, Himachal Pradesh, Panjab, Chandigarh and Haryana—could enter into responsible understandings to lend their armed and specialized police forces to each other for dealing with existing/arising internal disturbances. Such accords would also enable the collaborating States to establish strong joint fronts for collectively combating the growingly threatening activities of the drug cartels and terror networks. Under the aegis of the NSP, once it is formulated, such inter-state agreements could be placed on more formal footings.

There is no basis for the State's belief that the entire responsibility for managing internal disorders vests only with the Union government. On the contrary, the States are expected to play an important role in maintaining public order. Also, besides coming to each other's aid, they must commit to providing strong support to the Union government in dealing with the management of national security. Such cohesion, which would need to be systematically promoted by the NSP, shall enhance the unity and integrity of our country and strengthen our democracy.

As past experience has repeatedly shown, internal disturbances are generated by varied elements and factors: by the activities of insurgents, militants, radical Islamic groups which are assisted by adversary foreign agencies, narco-terror networks, anti-national and subversive elements, etc. The unfettered activities of the criminal nexus between politicians, public servants and organized crime and mafia networks also have the potential of generating serious disrubances.[4]

It has been seen that disorders also arise: (i) when partisan political groups seek to polarize and divide society on communal lines (as has happened many times since 1947), and (ii) when the frustration and anger of the neglected elements of society compels them to take to violence for having their demands met. In this context, it is important that the States, besides effectively enforcing law and order, also devote very special attention for promoting and assuring the welfare of the poverty stricken segments of our people. Towards this end, every development scheme/programme which is intended to promote the welfare of the neglected and oppressed segments of the population shall require to be implemented with promptitude, efficiency and honesty.

Maintenance of public order and an environment of normalcy is essential for the sustained growth and development of the country; it is also required for the effective functioning of the military apparatus, particularly when, in any emergency, there are movements of troops from the cantonments to the frontiers. Any disturbance in the hinterland would not only delay and endanger such movements but also threaten the military's lines of communication. This concern, of the connectivity between internal and external security, and the high responsibility of the States to maintain public order, would need to be particularly reckoned in the internal security doctrine which would be a vital element of the architecture of a well harmonized NSP, based on entirely apolitical understandings between the States and the Union. It needs being reiterated: internal security will be effectively managed only when the MHA and its agencies work in continuing, close and meaningful coordination with the State governments and their agencies.

II

I now turn to national defence or the arena of external security management: India's defence policy is to protect the country against all external threats and to deter and defeat aggression. India does not seek to wage war to conquer and occupy the territory of any country. It aspires to enjoy friendly and peaceful relations with its neighbours and all other countries.

Since Independence, Pakistan has waged and lost four wars against India: in 1947–8, 1965, 1971 and 1999. Our ill-prepared Army suffered defeat in the 1962 conflict with China. In the late-1980s India chose to intervene in the ethnic disturbances in northern Sri Lanka and deployed the Indian Peace Keeping Force (IPKF) in that country. This venture was unsuccessful as it was not based on clearly conceived politico–military objectives and also because of inadequate planning.

After 1962, we have had no war with China. However, our eastern neighbour has, over the years, built very strong fortifications along and across its disputed borders with India. For the past several years, China has been perpetrating military confrontations across the LAC which have generated continuing tension along the frontiers.

As regards our western neighbour, Pakistan: it has been continuing its proxy war in J&K for over three decades in pursuit of its unceasing campaign to seize Kashmir, and its radical networks are forever engaged in attempting to spread terror activities in our country.

We do not have a known national defence doctrine on the basis of which the working of the entire defence apparatus could be systematically organized to ensure that it works effectively and to its full potential. It has also not been so far possible for the higher defence management to get the Army, Navy and Air Force to work collectively for the systemic development of a truly powerful joint war fighting machinery.

Over the years, the three defence services have followed their own growth paths and developed largely as per the experience and instincts of their successive chiefs. The Defence Services have not been amenable to undertaking joint planning for preparing fully integrated 5 to 10 year defence plans which would enable the military to develop the capacity to deliver a collective knockout punch to the adversary. Consequently, in the years past, there has been hardly any worthwhile long-term thinking and the defence plans, such as they have been, have continued to be largely an agglomeration of three separate, Service-wise approaches. The MoD has been generally approving the disparate recommendations received from the chiefs of the three Services, even though these may not have been well conceived. Over the years this has led to extremely worrying gaps in the country's defence preparedness, besides leading to sub-optimal utilization of scarce financial resources, costly overlaps and duplication of expenditures.

In the past over seven decades, the gaps in the functioning of the MoD may be attributed, inter-alia, to the fact that most of the political personalities who have helmed this ministry in the years gone by have not had the time, and perhaps also rather limited interest, in acquiring sufficient knowledge about the functioning of the military, especially its operational aspects. Another telling reason: the IAS officers appointed as Defence Secretaries have been given extremely insufficient tenures, never more than two years and a few months; also, some of them may not have had the advantage of any earlier exposure to functioning in the security management arena. Furthermore, the other civilian officers deployed in the MoD, drawn from various All India and Central Services, also serve for limited tenures of 4 to 5 years. In view of these serious constraints, the MoD has not been able to build and sustain a dynamic body of specialized knowledge which would contribute towards better understanding and a more robust handling of military matters.

Following India's defeat in the 1962 conflict with China an enquiry was held to identify the causes of this debacle. The Henderson Brooks–Bhagat Report (1963) provided a very telling overview of the failures on various fronts. Regrettably, this report, classified 'top secret', has remained locked up for over six decades now. I had recommended that this document should be declassified[5] and made available to the three Service Headquarters and to the heads of all the military training institutions. However, the government faltered and left this matter hanging. Subsequent governments have also failed to muster courage.

After the Kargil War, the Union government set up the Kargil Review Committee (1999) to *'recommend such measures as are considered necessary to safeguard national security against such intrusions'* (referring to the Pak aggression in Kargil, which led to the war). Based on the recommendations of this Committee, the Union government, with the objective of strengthening national security, set up four Task Forces to recommend reforms in the functioning of Intelligence, Defence Management, Border Management and Internal Security. These task forces, comprising experienced veterans, made wide ranging recommendations. Regrettably, all the accepted reforms have not been implemented as yet.

Among the major recommendations made by the Task Force on Defence Management, the government agreed with those relating to the establishment of a Strategic Forces Command and the Andaman Nicobar Tri-Service Command. However, there was no agreement about creating the post of Chief of Defence Staff (CDS).

In the two decades and more which have elapsed since the Kargil Review Committee Report (1999), very significant changes have taken place in the geopolitical environment in India's neighbourhood and across the world. The continuing military situation along the LOC with Pakistan and the LAC with China, the Russia–Ukraine war and the consequential global developments, have generated multiple concerns, which include economic and other challenges for India. If the evolving scenario does not get peacefully settled soon enough, compulsions may arise for India to increase its military spending, much more than it has already done, which would impact the resources available for our developmental programmes.

The present Union government, which has been taking considerable interest in strengthening the country's security, has not so far committed to formulating an NSP, which would provide a known basis for evolving durable frameworks for internal, external and holistic national security management. However, it has moved determinedly forward on several fronts, among which reference may be made to the following:

(i) The status of the National Security Advisor (NSA) has been elevated. The present incumbent, who reports to the Prime Minister, has been accorded ministerial status. He steers the functioning of the National Security Council Secretariat (NSCS) which, by all accounts, has very considerably grown in size, resources and authority. The NSA now also chairs the Defence Planning Committee (DPC), which has the three Service Chiefs as its members (the DPC was earlier steered by the Defence Minister). The chiefs of IB, Research and Analysis Wing and other agencies also report to him.

(ii) The post of CDS was created and filled up (January 2020), initially by appointing a retiring Army chief and, later, by a retired Army Commander.

(iii) A new Department of Military Affairs (DMA) was created (January 2020) and placed under the charge of the CDS. The DMA deals with all personnel and other matters relating to the functioning of the three Services.

In so far as the charge of DMA is concerned, it would do well to bear in mind that in our parliamentary democracy the supervision, control and direction of the Defence Services vests with the elected political representative, the Defence Minister, and it is the PM who has the ultimate responsibility for all strategic decisions. There cannot be any deviation from this constitutional precept, which must form the bedrock of all reforms in the defence sector.

The post of CDS, who serves as the Principal Military Adviser to the Defence Minister, was created with the specific objective of improving coordination and effectiveness among the three Services by integrating their combat capabilities, to enable them to become capable of effectively launching joint operations.

The CDS has been given the rank of Secretary to the Government of India and placed in charge of the DMA, which has been created by taking away almost the entire work earlier done by the Defence Secretary. There is no basis whatsoever for the CDS to be burdened with this work, which would leave him no time for learning and discharging the essential duties for which he was appointed. From my own experience of working as Defence Secretary for over three years, I can say that the Secretary DMA's charge entails seven to eight hours daily desk work, relating to his secretarial responsibilities. Furthermore, the work relating to the selection, appointment, transfer and promotion of Service officers of Major General and above rank (and equivalent in the other two Services) requires to be processed under civilian oversight. The CDS must be relieved of the responsibility of functioning as Secretary DMA, so that he can discharge the duties for which he was appointed.

The first CDS was strongly committed to introducing jointness in the working of the Defence Services. However, before any headway could be made in this direction, he initiated hurried efforts to re-organize the functioning of the three Services by seeking to substitute their existing 18 Operational Commands by 5 integrated tri-Service

Theatre Commands: possibly two for the Army, one each for the Navy and the Air Force, and the fifth being the Strategic Force Command. While this move met with murmurs within the Navy, the Air Force publicly expressed its unhappiness over the proposed 'theatre-ization' concept, perhaps also irked by a media report that the CDS secretariat viewed the Army as the 'primary' service and the Air Force as a 'support' service.

I have referred to the aforesaid incident of contrariness among the Services to re-emphasize the high risk involved in continuing with the past practice of important national security related issues being hastily decided on ad-hoc considerations. It is of high importance to ensure that, before introducing any changes in the existing defence management apparatus the proposed re-organization plan should be based on a sound doctrinal approach which has been thoroughly discussed among all the stakeholders and a broad consensus achieved. The implementation process should commence only after the Union government has accorded formal approval to all the proposed changes, which are supported by all the stakeholders.

The CDS has not been vested with any operational authority. He will be able to perform fruitfully only after the entire range of vital Command and Staff issues relating to his role and responsibility, vis-à-vis the existing and the proposed hierarchical structures in the Services, have been fully and harmoniously settled. There must be total clarity about who will do what, under whose direction and be answerable to whom in the re-organized set-up. Until these issues are fully resolved, the present role and responsibility of the Chiefs of the three Services shall need to remain undisturbed and the Chiefs of Staff Committee should also continue to perform its designated role, dealing with all the matters placed before it and also looking beyond.

In the arena of defence reform: among the issues which require urgent, close and systematic attention, the most crucial challenge relates to the need for the three Services to lose no further time in commencing unwavering steps to achieve 'jointness' and gearing up for training, planning and operating collectively. For the attainment of this vital objective, it is necessary to replace the existing single-Service oriented training courses by Joint Services Command and Staff training programmes which would be provided at Joint Services Academies of Military Training and Education. Such courses, for collectively training officers of the three Services and preparing them for undertaking joint plans to conduct joint operations, shall inescapably need to be based on the concepts and strategies ingrained in the Joint War Fighting Doctrine which, necessarily, would need to be developed with most careful thought and intensive discussions between the three Services and all the other stakeholders.

The syllabi of the training to be provided at the Joint Services Command and Staff Training Academies should include, inter-alia, adequate learning about the history of India's freedom struggle; Constitution of India; functioning of the Executive, Legislature and Judiciary; the challenges relating to the achievement of rapid economic growth which secures reduction of poverty and equitable distribution of wealth.

In the rather unlikely eventuality of there being a lack of consensus among the Services to train, plan and operate collectively, the Union government should not hesitate to enact suitable legislation for securing this crucial objective.

Besides undertaking pragmatic reforms in the functioning of the defence apparatus, it would do well to recognise that there is close connectivity between the satisfactory functioning of the administrative machinery of our country and the safeguarding of its security. As past experience has shown: inefficiency, unaccountability and corruption in governance create wide openings for the breakdown of law and order, public disturbances and threats to national security, both from within and beyond the country.

It is of great importance that all required steps are taken to sustain an environment in which each of three organs of the Constitution perform their roles satisfactorily and harmoniously. Towards this end it shall be necessary to see that the unfettered functioning of pivotal national institutions, both statutory and constitutional, is effectively safeguarded and they are immunized from any kind of political interference or unlawful pressure. It is equally important that these institutions[6] are manned and steered by personnel of the highest competence and unimpeachable integrity. In this context, the NSP would need to provide for the promotion of good governance and the protection of critical national institutions from any manner of interference or politicization.

The Union government would be able to enormously increase the national strength if it takes appropriate initiatives for establishing strong Union–State relations, particularly in the arena of national security management. The NSP would need to advise the broad framework of security-related understandings among the States and between the States and the Union and, based on such an enlarged canvass, the MHA must systematically strive to establish vibrant links with the States, gain their trust, and encourage them to take decisions which serve the national interest.

As mentioned earlier, following upon the recommendations of the Kargil Review Committee Report, the Union government had established four Task Forces to make recommendations for strengthening national security. Among the many recommendations contained in the Report of the Task Force on Internal Security[7], based on my experience of working in the Home and Defence ministries for nearly a decade, I had pointed to the need for creating a pool of willing and interested officers—drawn from the civil, police, military, diplomacy, science, technology, engineering, space, finance, banking and various other services—who could be provided specialized training in identified areas to create a dedicated cadre from which appointments would be made for manning the posts in the Home and Defence ministries. This proposal was approved after extensive discussion in the Group of Ministers (GoM),[8] which went to the extent of even recommending higher remuneration for such trained personnel, as a reward for working in an important arena. Regrettably, the implementation of this decision[9] was subverted by vested interests.

The aforesaid decision of the GoM to build a pool of trained personnel for manning posts in the security management arena was taken over two decades ago. Since then our security environment has become far more worrisome. In my view it would be unwise to continue with the belief that internal and external security management related ministries and all the national security related agencies can be reliably run by personnel of disparate backgrounds who are appointed to serve on deputation tenures for limited periods of 4–5 years. At this juncture, I would suggest that the Union government would do well to take the bold decision of establishing a National Security Administration Service (NSAS) whose specially trained cadres would be deployed for running the pan-India Union–State security management apparatus, which requires to be expanded very significantly.

The NSAS cadres would promote continuity, efficiency and trustworthiness and, over time, contribute towards helping the States to gain a deeper understanding of issues relating to national security and also enable them to recognize the enormous advantages of their working with each other and with the Union government, for safeguarding the sovereignty of our country.

India has land and sea borders of nearly 23,000 km., 1,400 islands, an EEZ of 2.37 mn. sq. km. and a growing population of over 1.4 billion, which comprises thousands of ethnic groups who practise almost all the world religions, speak hundreds of dialects and languages as their mother tongues and have vastly differing socio–religious–cultural traditions, some of which are embedded in thousands of years of recorded history.

The NSP would need to recognize that the unbound diversity of our multi-religious, multi-lingual and multicultural people carries within it the seeds of inherent differences which, if not handled with the required sensitivity by the governance apparatus of the Union and the States, could lead to disagreements, disputes, violent conflicts and large scale disturbances in the country.

The State governments are closest to the people they govern and, as such, are intimately aware of the cultural and religious sensitivities of the various communities whose welfare they are mandated to promote. The NSP would need to focus on the high responsibility of the States not only to maintain peace and normalcy but to also provide good governance.

I would conclude by reiterating that it is the high responsibility of the Union and the States to work very closely together to imbue all our people with national fervour and make every citizen aware of his duty to safeguard the unity, integrity and sovereignty of India.

The NSP, evolved in meaningful consultations with the States, will promote the Rule of Law and the Constitution and the national security management apparatus, founded on doctrines derived from a truly apolitical NSP, will deter and successfully counter all threats to the country.

There must be no further delay in formulating the NSP.

NOTES

1. In 1992–3, when the Army made a proposal to raise a new infantry force, the Rashtriya Rifles, for meeting its growing commitments on the domestic front, I had (while serving as the then Defence Secretary) advised that a longer term view should be taken and, instead, the MHA should be provided with additional forces which are trained by the Army. As the MHA was not interested in this debate, the Army's proposal was approved.

2. For the past several decades there have been repeated protestations about the violation of human rights by Army units deployed in the disturbed areas. There have also been continuing agitations, particularly in the Northeast states, for the withdrawal of the Armed Forces (Special Powers) Act (which grants special powers to the Indian Armed Forces to maintain public order in areas declared 'disturbed' under the Disturbed Areas [Special Courts] Act) and, besides, scores of petitions in the higher courts for action being taken against the offenders.

3. An objective study of the situation leading up to Operation Blue Star would clearly establish that there was a serious

failure of the state government to timely and effectively deal with the arising problem. Furthermore, it would also become clear that certain political interests in the Government of India were working to dilute/subvert the Panjab Chief Minister's hard-line approach in this matter. Later, when the conflict had enlarged and become unmanageable, the State and even the Central police forces were not considered trustworthy to deal with the fast spreading conflagration. This led to rushing in the Army, which launched Operation Blue Star. It took well over a decade to contain the turmoil, which caused enormous human and economic losses and an unbridgeable cleavage among the communities.

4. The serial bomb blasts which devastated the erstwhile Bombay in March 1993 and, later, led to untold communal violence, killings and losses is an unforgettable episode, perpetrated by the mafia networks of Dawood Ibrahim and gang. On Prime Minister Narasimha Rao's direction I had (while functioning as the Union Home Secretary) furnished a report (since referred to as the 'Vohra Committee Report', October 1993; contained in 'RIGHT TO INFORMATION', published by Lok Shakti Abhiyan, Jawaharlal Nehru University, New Delhi) which had brought out, inter-alia, the sinister connectivity between politicians–public servants–organized crime mafia/syndicates and how this unwholesome nexus had progressively enhanced its influence, money and muscle power to succeed in virtually establishing a parallel government, pushing the state apparatus into irrelevance. This report pointed to the need for immediate steps being taken to establish a machinery for effectively dealing with the threatening activities of the growing politico-mafia nexus. Three decades have since elapsed. By all accounts, the criminal nexus has grown significantly and extended its lethal power and reach.

5. Unfortunately, the secrecy syndrome has also affected other areas of functioning. In 2001, years after my retirement,

Defence Minister George Fernandes asked me to chair a committee and advise regarding the publication of Military Histories of the 1947–8, 1962, 1965 and 1971 wars (these histories had been finalized during my tenure as Defence Secretary, but had remained under 'secret' classification). In my report to the Raksha Mantri, I had recommended the declassification and urgent publication of all these four war histories. My recommendation was accepted but, for unknown reasons, these histories were not released for publication for many years to come. I continue to believe that lifting the bar on the Henderson Brooks–Bhagat Report and the timely publication of the military histories would have engendered an environment which would have compelled reforms in the functioning of the defence apparatus and, besides, enabled generations of upcoming military officers, undergoing training in various academies, to learn valuable lessons from the failures in India's past military engagements.

6. Illustratively: Union Public Service Commission; Comptroller & Auditor General; Election Commission of India; Central Bureau of Investigation; Enforcement Directorate; Central Vigilance Commission; Central Information Commission; National Investigation Agency; Intelligence Bureau; R&AW; Joint Intelligence Committee; NSCS and all the agencies which function under its control.

7. This Task Force, chaired by me, furnished its report to the Union Government in September 2000.

8. The GoM, chaired by Deputy Prime Minister and Home Minister K.L. Advani, included the Defence, Finance and External Affairs Ministers as its members.

9. 'Report of the Group of Ministers on National Security', 2000, p. 56, para 4.05.

II

India's National Security and the Way Ahead

Sujan R. Chinoy

Let me begin with what I regard as a key national security challenge. The first and foremost for me is for India to achieve rapid economic growth. I know this is a little contrarian—it is normal for us to refer to national security in terms of either hard power or smart power, or sharp power, as they put it now, beyond soft power. But for me, the essential challenge here is economic growth, economic strength in absolute as well as relative terms. And in relative terms, I would use as a foil, a benchmark, the rapidity with which China has pulled away from India. We were virtually at the same level in 1980, with per capita GDP at the same level, and by 2020, we have seen that they are roughly five times bigger. By 2022, they're likely to be six times bigger.

All that we do with regard to our national security challenges, the manner in which we assess them, the manner in which we develop structures and resources to address them will also fundamentally depend on our economic strengths. Therefore, rapid and inclusive economic growth is fundamental, and it requires a stable and peaceful periphery. And we also need to ensure that we are able to take our own decisions through strategic autonomy. Our role in recent years has been strengthened, no doubt, and our democratic institutions, our potential, our military capabilities and resolute political will are on display to the rest of the world.

By being a non-permanent member of the UN Security Council, we may be able to shape the global environment a little better. And there is a certain dynamism which we see today, through the COVID-19 pandemic, in terms of our emergence as a central player in regard to healthcare as well. But the context is also very important. This is, after all, a world which is in great flux—there is continuing uncertainty, the fragility of the international compact cannot be over-emphasized. It has been further weakened by the pandemic. Multilateralism as we all know is a cliché, to say that it has not lived up to its promise. And the politics of the pandemic, the politics of the trade and technology war that preceded the pandemic, the weaponization of trade and technology have also taken global attention away from key developmental issues in the context of US–China friction. This has been immensely disruptive.

There is obviously a situation, a kaleidoscopic situation, in which we have seen the division now falling into place in terms of trade, technology, tenets and values, narratives, and, of course, the systems through which we seek to develop ourselves: whether it's going to be the liberal trading order, or whether it will be the authoritarian trading order, or whether it will be capitalism or state capitalism. All these options are before us today. And we are looking at developing new resilient supply chains as well, which is a priority as the pandemic has shown us, but it was the case before as well. The fact is that if you are overly reliant on supply chains emanating from a certain part of the world, then you are likely to be gamed. China has been able to game the system well.

In the post-pandemic era, the greatest challenge will be equitable economic growth and sufficient healthcare. The post-pandemic world is going to be characterized by further economic competition—no doubt about that. And the consideration of geopolitics and geo-economics will be inseparable. Military competition is on the rise. And for us, the challenge is going to be to find the resources for this military competition that seems to be looming ahead of us in Asia in the future.

We are currently not part of the Regional Comprehensive Economic Partnership (RCEP). We have to ensure that our export performance really backs us up in terms of ensuring our place at the head table in terms of our economic performance. In the region, again, we've seen violence in Afghanistan, but we have been brought to be seated at the head table in terms of dialogue mechanism. That is an improvement in terms of what we can do to alter and moderate behaviour in Afghanistan. But the tensions around us, whether in the Gulf of Hormuz, whether in eastern Ladakh today, elsewhere on the Line of Actual Control (LAC) tomorrow, are expected to continue. And we will have to contend with that alongside the challenges of climate change, energy, food security, etc. These will all be centre stage. Terrorism for us continues to be an albatross around our neck. And we will be dealing with state and non-state actors in a fractured world.

The rise of China, of course, has altered the balance of power in Asia. Whether it will be an Asian century or a Chinese century remains to be seen. In West Asia, again, we have witnessed flux. Russia, I believe, is at a very important point of inflection. And the protests there are likely to alter the situation dramatically in the years to come. Of course, Russia could emerge suddenly as an ally of the United States, or at least maintain neutrality. And if Russia flips over, the geostrategic map of Asia will change overnight. We've seen that happen in the past in the early 1990s.

Now, as regards the Biden administration. We have seen once again that it has committed itself to multilateralism, alliance partnerships, and as a matter of fact, to the geopolitical contestation with China as well. And this is quite evident in all the statements made at the highest level. So, while we are looking at this broad scenario, I'm currently focusing on the external environment, leaving it to other eminent speakers to take a deeper dive into internal security, or the reform of various national security structures.

As for disengagement at the LAC, there is no gain saying the fact that bilateral differences are best negotiated from a position of strength as was done at Pangong Tso. Yet we have to maintain high vigil. A ceasefire on the Line of Control (LoC) is welcome. But it's not an insurance against Pak-sponsored terrorism. If anything, I believe that the Deep State may not cooperate fully with either the political leadership or the Army top brass. The temptation for terror groups to disrupt this process will always be there, and we need to guard against cross-border infiltration of the type that we see through tunnels, for example, in the Jammu sector and in Panjab as well. It only takes one or two people to cross over with very insidious motives to cause mayhem in the country.

The coup in Myanmar is a fresh challenge. And our low-key approach is advisable. We have done well to keep ourselves relatively in the background—we cannot afford to make the mistake that was made way back in 1988. The risk of refugees coming across whether Rohingyas or other ethnic minorities, out of Myanmar proper or Bangladesh, is likely to increase.

The rise of China, of course, is the big question. Its unilateralism and aggression has fuelled a kind of contestation across the Indo–Pacific. In my view, China's rise has been disruptive right from the very beginning. It was disruptive first for China itself between 1949 and 1979. That 30-year period was nothing but unmitigated upheavals and disasters, albeit internal. But it also had remote ramifications for the region at large. During the next 30-year period, from 1979 to 2009, the Chinese found their sweet spot with a Midas touch when everything they did on the economic front led to growth and development. It is the third 30-year period that we find ourselves in, and that has been rather tumultuous.

After the global financial and economic crisis, China has become ever more aggressive, and not the least with the arrival of Xi Jinping. China has its own Monroe Doctrine of sorts which the Japanese followed in the 1930s.

Wilhelmine Germany too had demonstrated that tendency. But neither of these two rising powers in the past were able to achieve their ends. Therefore, there is no guarantee that China would be able to do the same.

Rising powers, and especially China, must therefore understand, the meaning of power and especially the limits of power. To what extent can power be exercised without inviting a backlash? I think this is where China has failed miserably. It has failed to convince the region of its rise, of its motives, of its intentions. It has failed to respect the sensitivities of others. It has expected the world to open up its markets but has failed to open up its own markets.

And so the challenge for us is to also deal with this kind of China in the future, beyond disengagement, beyond interim peace on the border. We have to look at the major trigger points that are likely to come up in the near future.

The year 2021 was an important one for China. In October the Party Congress marked its 100th anniversary. The year 2035 is another very important inflection point in terms of the modernization of the military. Finally, the most important, of course, is 2050, when the Chinese want to realize their 'China Dream' and 'national rejuvenation'. And without the integration of Taiwan, without the integration of territories which China claims, it is hardly possible for China to claim that the 'dream' has been realized.

Therefore, I believe that between now and 2050, there will be several trigger points for which we have to be on the lookout.

Disengagement is important: I think the criticism about vacating the Kailash Range was unwarranted. We should handle each of these sectors *sui generis*.

There are several issues in our relations with China. The first is territory, as is well known. Differences over the boundary and the LAC; a proxy problem in terms of the China-Pakistan Economic Corridor (CPEC) passing through contested territory in Gilgit–Baltistan; the land grab in Shaksgam. And then there is technology, which relates to AI, cyber security, etc. Rapid military advances are also an issue.

In trade, there is adverse trade balance. There are differences in tenets in terms of democracy here versus authoritarianism there. There is the issue of transparency in terms of the lack of clarity about their intentions in South Asia, and especially in the Indian Ocean region. Above all, the multilateral space for us to cooperate with China is shrinking. As such, there is a trust deficit.

There is, for instance, a complete disruption in the region as a result of the geo-economic forces unleashed by China, which are redefining the geostrategic landscape as well. China seeks an expulsion of the US from the periphery. But the US, like France and the UK, has long been an integral part of the region, and the Indo-Pacific, of course, is a much more inclusive concept as compared to the Asia-Pacific region.

In the Indo-Pacific, I believe the Quad is gradually acquiring form and substance. Creating resilient supply chains is easier said than done because the experience of this so-called shift out of China has not been very positive. Very few companies have actually come to India. More have gone to Southeast Asia. But we must continue to strengthen our ties with the Quad. In my view, the Quad needs to have a security-oriented core and an inclusive exoskeleton which focuses more on developmental issues. But without generous alternatives, the region will continue to be attracted, as moths to a flame, literally, for an eventual burnout through China's developmental finance.

The US, in my view, needs to take the lead but avoid great power exceptionalism, including FONOPs against partners, and the US should also do more in the Taiwan Strait. Many are not aware that the US has not sent a single carrier battle group to the Taiwan Strait since the USS Kitty Hawk in 2007. Yes, it is true that the USS Theodore Roosevelt recently went to the South China Sea, but it sailed through the Bashi Strait and not through the Taiwan Strait. A guided missile destroyer did go through the Taiwan Strait in early February 2021, but then, it was not a carrier battle task force.

I think the Quad nations also must be encouraged to work more closely with us to depict our boundaries correctly. Currently, none of the other three depict India's boundaries correctly. We should also do more in terms of opening up the Andaman and Nicobar Islands and try to cooperate more in terms of the Malacca Strait patrols on the other side of the Malacca.

Pakistan, once again, remains a cross that we have to bear, a burden that has remained so for many decades. It is a huge security challenge and the epicentre of terrorism. I think we need to keep up the pressure with regard to our zero tolerance for terrorism. And we have to keep in mind that this tandem with China is likely to remain unchanged. If anything, it is growing stronger as the Pakistanis pull away from the Americans. Pakistan and China are likely to work in tandem to undermine the region in the long term, and we must keep that in mind.

We need not pay too much heed to the UNMOGIP (UN Military Observer Group in India and Pakistan). It has no sunset clause. But I believe it is irrelevant and outdated and India has done well to reduce its facilities.

Cyber threats are very important. We are, in fact, currently living in a phase where everybody, due to COVID-19, has shifted to online platforms. We are one of the biggest targets in the world today, as we have seen recently in the context of the Maharashtra electricity transmission company facing major problems. We need to work harder to prevent cyber attacks, reduce vulnerability, create the right kind of test-beds for our algorithms, minimize damage in terms of data theft, and promote R&D in AI. Future wars will rely much more on such advanced digital and stand-off weapons technologies as well.

Fake narratives are a major national security challenge today, whether on Article 370 or the Citizenship Amendment Act (CAA). There is a growing tendency for domestic opposition to forge a tandem with external forces. The challenge in terms of achieving *atmanirbharta* in defence also remains. There are budgetary constraints. We have done well to provide our armed forces with robust means to deal with the immediate challenge in eastern Ladakh, and this has probably taken the Chinese also by surprise. The absolute speed with which this was done was to equip our armed forces. But India still remains a net importer of arms, and this has been the case for far too long. We need to do much more by way of involving the private sector in order to get over this particular lacuna.

I will end with internal security which we cannot afford to ignore. Management of inter-faith issues, the Left-wing extremism threat which has abated but is still very potent, counter-radicalization strategies, developmental challenges in J&K and the Northeast, and above all, national security and military reforms are crucial. And more important than anything else, as Mr N.N. Vohra mentioned, is the creation of necessary human resources that will specialize in and provide the capacity for dialogue to build the necessary consensus and support the structures that are required for this particular jointness.

III

India's National Security Challenges
An Overview

Arun Prakash

A t the outset, I must state my conviction, that while excessive focus on systemic deficiencies and shortcomings in a democracy can be bad for public morale, self-delusion is a luxury we can no longer afford, because this 'national malaise' has endangered our national security in the past.

The three grave crises that overtook India in 2020— a pandemic, an economic downturn and a military confrontation—are going to have far-reaching consequences, not just for the country's security, but even more so, for its long-term development and overall growth. While an economy, contracting in real terms, will aggravate many socio-economic problems, shrinking defence budgets may be inadequate to sustain even current force levels, leave alone modernizing or re-equipping our military.

Given this dismal prospect, it will take 'out-of-the-box' thinking and adroit economic management to set the country back on the path to recovery. During this interregnum, it will be the military's task to uphold the nation's sovereignty and territorial integrity. Our current predicaments, thus, provide an opportunity for military thinkers and security experts to find innovative responses to security challenges—current and foreseeable.

Resorting to application of force, or waging of war, must remain a measure of last resort because even the victor pays a heavy price in the ultimate reckoning. Given India's unenviable situation of being a nuclear power, sandwiched between two nuclear-armed adversaries, this question assumes grave dimensions with international implications.

The decision to go to war should come only after statesmen and diplomats have exhausted all other avenues of dispute resolution. However, the view that outbreak of hostilities signals the failure of statesmanship, and that soldiers must be given a 'free hand' to wage war is flawed. We must never forget Prussian strategist Clausewitz's admonition that, "War does not have its own logic and purpose. It is nothing but continuation of policy with other means.' Also, his advice that, 'The soldier must always be subordinate to the statesman; the conduct of war is the latter's responsibility ...'

If war is, indeed, a political enterprise, it must be waged with the aim of eliminating the *casus belli* and achieving a stable and enduring peace. This places two onerous responsibilities on the country's political leadership: firstly, to lay down, for the military, clear aims for which war is being fought, and secondly, to specify the desired 'end-state' to be achieved before 'war-termination'.

Unfortunately, in India, these stipulations have been disregarded time and again, and by this omission, the political leadership seems to have shrugged off a heavy responsibility. This responsibility requires the government to ensure that the budget and military capabilities available are commensurate with the threats that the armed forces are being asked to counter or eliminate. This 'ends-ways-means' conundrum has never been addressed by the politician and the reason is not far to seek.

India's post-Independence political establishment, of all hues, has exhibited detachment from vital issues related to national security; invariably according priority to the pursuit of politics and fighting/winning elections. Consequently, India alone, among major powers, has suffered from the lack of an institutional process which generates defence reviews, policy white papers and national security strategies.

Not only has this serious void inhibited our capacity to predict threats and evolve responses, it has engendered an 'ostrich-syndrome' that has engendered false optimism and prevented the funding of requisite military capability. Lacking authentic assessments, both of own capabilities and of adversary intentions, India's civilian leadership has, since 1947, failed to strategize and often erred in decision-making.

To this lacuna have been added the shortcomings in the working of our Ministry of Defence (MoD), manned entirely by civil servants and presided over by ministers preoccupied with the politics of parliament, constituency and unending elections. This has left the management of the armed forces and the MoD's decision-making in the hands of a transient civilian bureaucracy, lacking adequate knowledge of national security as well as military technology.

This combination of political indifference and bureaucratic neglect has resulted in the MoD's failure to exercise oversight and provide guidance to several organizations critical to national security. These include, the Defence Research and Development Organization (DRDO), Defence PSUs and the

Ordinance Factories Board. Consequently, one of the biggest security challenges before us today is how to overcome our abject dependence on imported military hardware and to kick-start overdue modernization of our armed forces. Programmes like Make in India and Atamanirbharta are welcome, but they too are dependent on the bureaucracy for implementation, and may take years to fructify.

Against the backdrop of these significant handicaps, India's handling of national security challenges has left much to be desired. The past decades saw successive security crises, catching India by surprise; unprepared and invariably in the reactive mode, with governments often exhibiting diffidence and lack of resolve.

All this changed on 29 September 2018, when the National Democratic Alliance (NDA) government deployed Special Forces to deliver a punitive strike on terrorist camps inside Pakistan, breaching the self-imposed taboo of earlier regimes. The February 2019 air-strike, on another terrorist facility in Pakistan, re-affirmed the government's resolve that cross-border terrorism would not go unpunished. While these decisive actions have earned well-deserved praise, two years down the line, it was not clear whether they were just 'one-off' events or signalled a new approach to national security.

This would have been an opportune moment to issue a security doctrine, which would provide guidelines for our own security forces, and send a clear message to neighbours that border transgressions—whether by military forces or by state-sponsored terrorists—would invite retribution. In my opinion, the absence of such a 'declaration of intent' continues to be seen as a lack of resolve on India's part, and has thus encouraged adventurism, both by Pakistan and by China. Witness the events of April–May 2020 in Eastern Ladakh.

China, in the midst of a pandemic, has reaffirmed its revanchist agenda by its actions in the Himalayas. However, it is quite clear that in spite of the overall military asymmetry and the active China–Pakistan nexus, Indian forces are ready to repel and punish any localized offensive by one or both. But there is also the reality that if general hostilities break out on our northern and western borders, the best that India can hope to achieve is a military stalemate.

Under these circumstances, as India prepares for the long haul, it must bring to bear all elements of its comprehensive national power against adversaries. That is the reason why attention has been focused on the maritime domain. Given our historic malady of 'sea-blindness', naval power has not always received its due in India—either as an instrument of diplomacy or of compellence and deterrence.

But a navalist school of thought has, of late, been advocating use of the Navy to not only reach out and seek mutually beneficial maritime partnerships, but also to exercise visible sea-control in the maritime neighbourhood. The stretch of Indian Ocean, from the Persian Gulf to Malacca Straits, hosts vital trade and energy sea-lanes, which constitute the economic 'jugular veins' of many nations including China. Regardless of buffer stocks, any disruption or delay of shipping traffic could upset China's economy, with consequent effects on industry and population.

The Indian Navy, despite parsimonious budgets, has emerged as a compact but professional and competent force, and India's fortunate maritime geography enables the peninsula to dominate the Indian Ocean. While zealously safeguarding the right to 'freedom of navigation', the Indian Navy can also exploit China's sea-lane vulnerability and use it as a 'pressure point' via threat of trade warfare. We must, however, bear in mind that the People's Liberation Army (PLA) Navy—which now outnumbers the US Navy—is backed by China's vast financial resources and the world's most prolific shipbuilding industry.

To conclude: Having fought five 'conventional' wars since 1947 and having engaged non-stop in low intensity conflict, much of it sponsored by neighbours, India's armed forces have imbibed a deep sense of 'territoriality.' This has engendered an inflexible doctrine which compels the Army to reflexively seek to place 'boots on the ground' everywhere. The roots of this mindset lie, substantially, in the unrealistic, resolutions passed by India's parliament undertaking to recover 'every inch of Indian territory' occupied by Pakistan and China.

It is against this backdrop that we need to introspect about our capacity to meet future security challenges of the twenty-first century. While the 'material' or 'hardware' shortcomings of our armed forces may be relatively easy to address, it is the intellectual challenge of evolving a long-term vision for India and its neighbourhood that will test the abilities of our national security decision-makers. Only when our politicians, diplomats, soldiers and bureaucrats are able to conceptualize such a vision, will they be able to articulate a long-overdue national security strategy for India.

It seemed that an auspicious beginning had been made in end-2019, with the creation of a Department of Military Affairs (DMA), as well as the post of a Chief of Defence Staff (CDS). This brightened India's prospect of achieving the long-sought-after goals of long-term integrated planning and interservice 'jointness', as well as 'civil-military integration'. There will, no doubt, be hurdles and pitfalls to be overcome on the way. Therefore, the prime minister's call at the Commanders' Conference, on 6 March 2021 for breaking down of 'civil-military silos,' and for transforming the Indian military into a 'future fighting force' was a most welcome pronouncement from the highest level of government.

IV

Internal Security

Ajay Sahni

B efore I start, I'd like to say that I agree very strongly with almost everything Admiral Arun Prakash has said. I think the crisis we have today is the failure to match our rhetoric and our vision, or what passes for vision in this country or our strategic projections, with our capacities, capabilities, budgets, and in fact, the entire chain that goes into creating a national muscle. We are in a peculiar situation when we look at the internal security environment today, where there are manifestations of traditional categories of violence, terrorism, insurgency falling very drastically, but leaving a state of extreme uncertainty, almost of instability, intact. While the movements themselves have collapsed, the causes, the dynamic that produced these movements seem to have been kept alive and in many cases been exacerbated.

To take a very quick overview of the numbers that we have seen over the last decades: in 2001, insurgencies and terrorism cost this country 5,504 lives. In 2020, we had a total fatality of 591 people killed in all categories: terrorists, civilians and security force personnel. Within this, in Kashmir too, terrorism has virtually collapsed, but it must be emphasized that while terrorism has virtually collapsed in Kashmir, we see a constant drumming up of hysteria. I will return to this and the motivations that go into creating this hysteria, this polarizing politics that characterizes everything in our environment today. Kashmir has gone from a peak of 4,011 fatalities in 2001 in a single year, down to just 321 fatalities in 2020 The same thing is seen in the Northeast, from a peak of 1,165 fatalities in 2003, down to just 27 fatalities in 2020. The Maoists, from a peak of 1,179 fatalities to 591 fatalities in 2020.

The scope of this violence has also diminished enormously. In terms of the number of districts affected in Kashmir, for instance, between 50 and 70 per cent of all violence, including terrorist and civil disorders like stone pelting, occurred over the period between 2017 and 2019, before the Article 370 intervention, in just 5 of 82 tehsils.

The same is true of the Maoist and Northeast insurgencies. We are seeing a virtual collapse of all insurgencies across the country. This having been said, I would like to emphasize that the security forces are the primary factor responsible for this collapse. It is the security forces and the intelligence establishment that have slowly eroded the capacity and capability of the adversaries. Some constructive developmental initiatives have filled some of these gaps, but not others. It is not the case that all areas which have been recovered by the security forces are seeing a comparable development. In fact, there are many areas that continue to face very significant neglect, but the security forces having done their jobs is only at the beginning. The security forces cannot defeat terrorism, cannot defeat an insurgency. They can contain it. What is required to defeat the insurgency, and Admiral Arun Prakash also talked about this, is the removal in classical warfare of the *casus belli*. That is a political factor.

It requires political wisdom, it requires political sagacity, and that is where I think the greatest lacuna exists in the contemporary Indian environment.

What we see instead of inclusive growth is non-inclusive growth. Admiral Chinoy also spoke of growth being the most important and emphasized inclusive growth. This non-inclusive growth excludes large segments of the population, while it enriches very small cabals in the country at this juncture. We have polarizing politics that exploits every division—communal, caste, regional, economic, class. All these are being pitted one against the other to create a sense of ferment, insecurity and fear across the country, which, at this juncture, we do not see reflected in the levels of violence, but it is a tremendous threat.

In the foreseeable future, and I am not even talking about the long-term future, we will see a rapid erosion of the integrity and autonomy of state institutions; a near complete breakdown of the separation of powers between institutions. Institutions are being subordinated to partisan political goals. Individuals, groups and parties are being targeted. There is a whole range of investigations and prosecutions. Even as insurgencies collapse, there is ongoing myth-making about urban Maoists, people being arrested for disagreeing with the government, branded terrorists, brought under the Unlawful Activities Prevention Act (UAPA), imprisoned for months, years, sometimes decades, in a process that I can only describe as punishment by trial. You don't need evidence; you just have to take a case and throw a 11,000- or 40,000-page chargesheet at the courts, name several hundred witnesses, and since it is supposed to be a very serious case of terrorism, bail will not be provided. Therefore, people can suffer years and decades of imprisonment without any serious evidence being produced against them at any stage of this process. Courts openly collude with state agencies to ignore the imperatives of minimal justice, of justice or principles that have been laid down by the Supreme Court, and which the Supreme Court itself ignores.

So, we must understand that this kind of neglect of all institutional norms, and a destruction of the independence of the various segments of government will eventually weaken the nation's capacities to respond to every crisis or to every challenge. This is a process that has been going on for decades, but has become far more intensive under the current regime.

What happens in the vacuum that are now being created? People on the street often have state support. We have seen humiliating, embarrassing, shameful incidents of collusion between state forces and criminals out on the streets. No nation can grow strong under a system that is being so completely corroded by hate and by a politics of polarization and separation between people.

Talk about economics. That is at the core of it all. We've talked about growth being the most important aspect of development. The pattern of growth is crucial, even lower rates of growth, which combine with sagacity and equity. During the COVID-19 pandemic in 2020, for instance, the Indian (rupee) billionaires increased their wealth by 35 per cent, even as the poor (lowest 50 per cent of the population) actually lost income. This growth helps no one. What is the character of growth that is going to help this country needs to be understood. Everyone speaks of the marriage of technology and state. But that is not enough. We talk about acquiring weapons from France or from the United States and we are an emerging great power. This is not what the sinews of a nation state are built on.

Great power is built on a chain. A chain that has the military industrial complex at its apex. But the military industrial complex is based on a much longer tail which is technology, science, education and human resource profiles. I'm afraid we fare disastrously on each of these parameters. We may talk about the many thousands of graduates, but in terms of our actual national capacities, there is 26 per cent participation in higher education in this country. And the quality of that higher education is abysmal in all but a small handful of institutions, which fortunately, or unfortunately, most of the gentlemen on this panel and most of our audience are likely to be drawn from. We have a very distorted view and believe we are all like this. But no, the quality and the scale of education in this country cannot provide you with the basis of scientific development, technological development and economic spread that is required to support a truly modernizing and emerging great power.

Nothing I'm saying is really extraordinary. Mr Vohra mentioned several committees, which had spoken of a specific security administration cadre. We are still in a situation where we spend INR 3 per capita per diem for the population on our state police forces—you cannot get a cup of tea for INR 5 on the streets. How are you going to become a great power when you do not invest in the fundamentals—in intelligence, in security, in justice?

I would like to reiterate what Admiral Arun Prakash said, that it is very easy to delude ourselves. There is chaos developing all across the world. The chaos can produce opportunities, but can also consume you. It is time to stop deceiving ourselves and commit ourselves to a true national reconstruction, which does not ignore an overwhelming proportion of the Indian population.

V

Managing Two Adversaries

Deependra S. Hooda

I'm going to focus quite narrowly on managing two adversaries, primarily China and Pakistan. There are many aspects to it, but because this is a discussion on national security, I will be talking about managing China and Pakistan from a security perspective.

Even from this perspective, if you ask 10 different people, they will have 10 different ideas about how to manage Pakistan and how to manage China. Therefore, in attempting to find an approach, I think the first thing we need to do is to answer two fundamental questions: first, what are our strategic objectives vis-à-vis Pakistan and China? Unfortunately, as Admiral Arun Prakash also pointed out, in the absence of any sort of clear political guidelines or a national security strategy that will lay these out, I think we have to start looking at what these national security objectives should be. So, do we go by the political rhetoric that our objectives are a return of occupied territories in Pakistan Occupied Kashmir (PoK), and a return of our territories that have been occupied by China in Aksai Chin, which will then require us to build offensive capabilities to meet these particular objectives? Or should we look at our strategic objectives in more modest terms? And when I say more modest terms, I mean that our security objectives should be in securing our current de facto borders, ensuring that there is no unilateral change on these borders by either country, and preventing cross-border terrorism emanating from Pakistan. With secure frontiers and secure borders, we can, as Ambassador Chinoy pointed out, go on with our economic development and, as Dr Ajay Sahni pointed out, an equitable economic development.

If we assume that these more modest objectives are what we should be looking at, then would a strategy of deterrence be more suitable for India? And in talking about a strategy of deterrence, I mean deterring Pakistan from carrying out cross-border violence and cross-border terrorism; deterring China from military coercion either along our territorial frontiers in the north or in the Indian Ocean in our maritime territories. Would therefore a strategy of deterrence be more suitable?

Let me clarify here that when I talk of a strategy of deterrence, it is not necessarily a defensive strategy. A strategy of deterrence relies on potential use of military force rather than the actual application of military force. A strategy of deterrence is also one which combines all elements of national power, economics, land power, maritime power and economic potential. All this is then combined with diplomacy in the strategy of deterrence.

A strategy of deterrence also does not make a clear distinction between peacetime and wartime. I do not think it correct or appropriate for us to say that there will be a clear dividing line between wartime and peacetime. We are seeing coercion along our borders, we are seeing cross-border terrorism, which is continuing during peacetime. We have recently seen how cyber threats can manifest themselves in peacetime. Therefore, we should have a more coherent strategy that is not only applicable during wartime but also during peace. We need a combination of all elements of national power, working throughout, irrespective of what the conditions are, to be able to pursue a policy of deterrence to deter Pakistan and China.

A strategy of deterrence is also one that takes a more nuanced approach to conflict. Thus, it takes into consideration, for example, how to react to local incidents. How do you handle escalation? Can escalation be controlled? Can we achieve a sense of victory at each stage of escalation? When we look at our overall strategic objectives and an overall strategy, these are issues that need to be debated much more. Unfortunately, in the absence of proper coherent structures for national security decision-making, and as Admiral Arun Prakash also pointed out, given the nature of civil-military cooperation that exists in India, I think we will have to review all our structures; we will have to review our policies and strategy.

The second fundamental question is should our strategy be diplomacy led or military led? I say this for a specific reason because of the manner in which we have been looking particularly to deal with Pakistan in the past few years. Let me also clarify here that a diplomacy led strategy does not necessarily rule out the use of military force. But it puts primacy on diplomacy, on economic measures, on sanctions, on international alliances, on international cooperation, etc. What we have seen in the past few years with Pakistan is that we seem to have relegated diplomacy to the background, and brought military activity and actions to the forefront. I think we need to honestly ask ourselves whether this strategy has succeeded and to what extent. Does an escalation or a military activation of two borders, both northern and western, serve India's strategic interests? And now, with an assertive China ready to use military force, would our diplomacy led strategy pay us better dividends? This, then, is the second fundamental question: what is the focus of our strategy against these two countries—military led or diplomacy led?

My final point is that any strategy, particularly a deterrence strategy, depends on three factors: communication, credibility and capability. In our communication, we must clearly state our national interest, and what our national red lines are. Particularly where China is concerned, we are extremely reticent and hesitant in clearly articulating these. It would have been much better, as everyone has pointed out, if we had a national security strategy that would lay down these red lines, these objectives, the national interests. If we are looking to be a potential global power, it is time that we shed this hesitation in articulating a national strategy that is sometimes seen as tying our hands or spoiling our relationships with our neighbours. The time for that has passed. So clear communication of our intent is what is needed.

Obviously, our actions must be credible. And here, I must point out that our actions against the People's Liberation Army (PLA) in Ladakh, and the way the three services have responded, has very significantly enhanced our credibility, not only as far as China is concerned but globally too. The fact that India has stood up has been a very credible response.

The issue again, as Admiral Arun Prakash has pointed out, is if we are consistent enough in our approach? He gave the example of two cross-border operations, one in 2016 and the other in Balakot in 2019. But is our approach consistent? Two months after Uri in 2016, we had the attack on Nagrota, and there was really no response from our side. So, are we doing this for extraneous considerations? Or are we following a consistent kind of approach in showing that India has a credible response to actions that doesn't suit its national interests?

Finally, I come to the issue of capability. Obviously, you can communicate anything and have all kinds of rhetoric, but the fact is that unless you have the capability that is in line with the threats that India faces, that is in line with our global ambitions, it will just look like empty words. In terms of capability, I want to point out that we need to do more, and we need to do different. When I say we need to do more, our current defence budget is insufficient for the kind of global ambitions that we have. It is not possible to modernize and build capability with the current state of the defence budget. I understand there are economic issues and problems, but there has to be some kind of balance. I'm afraid that as we go ahead in the future, the disparity that already exists between India and China is going to grow manifold. I'm afraid that resisting coercion from China is going to become more and more difficult. We have a great advantage in the maritime space, but as Admiral Arun Prakash has pointed out, the PLA Navy is already the largest in the world in terms of number of battleships. And it is investing very heavily in the navy. So, will our advantages in the Indian Ocean get further diluted as we go ahead?

Why I said we also need to do things differently is because I think we are investing too much in legacy military systems, ships, guns, tanks, etc., and there is just not enough focus on modern warfighting tools. Again, this was also pointed out by Ambassador Chinoy. We are not investing enough in cyber, space, information warfare, electronic warfare, artificial intelligence, robotics, unmanned systems, etc. So even within the military, we need to introspect on how we need to do things. Even if the budget is available, as they say, unless the doctrines, processes, procedures and the kind of capabilities needed are clear, then even money is not going to help.

Many people ask this question: how will a two-front war actually play out in case we have to fight one? It is very difficult to make any predictions. After World War I broke out in 1914, the most popular phrase was that it will be over by Christmas. It went on for the next four years. So while we can't predict, I think it would be safe to say that in a two-front scenario, India is going to be extremely hard pressed. There is no doubt about that. Therefore, all our efforts, strategic thinking, management of adversaries, and how we go ahead must concentrate on the approach that we must deter the possibility of both adversaries coming together.

VI

Air Power in Coercion and Limited War Scenario

Arjun Subramaniam

I will try to offer some perspectives, both traditional and contrarian, on the employment of air power, not just in the limited conflict scenario, but also in environments that we are very familiar with—that is what I'd like to call 'less than war situations', situations that call for deterrence, situations that call for coercion, and a demonstration of strength without actually engaging in warfighting.

Let me put on my historian's hat and explore how the Indian strategic community as a whole has looked at air power since Independence when, from 1947 to 1971, the Indian Air Force and Indian air power were primarily seen as a progressively improving instrument of warfighting. But it was only in 1971 that air power emerged as an instrument of just more than warfighting, as an instrument of coercion and one that can hasten the psychological collapse of an adversary. I'm talking about the various actions in the eastern theatre that accelerated the collapse of the Pakistan Army in Bangladesh. I'm talking about the Tangail airdrop, I'm talking about the strike on the governor's house, and those multiple operations of vertical envelopment that were orchestrated by two very accomplished joint practitioners General Sagat Singh and Group Captain Chandan Singh. So the seeds of coercion were sown in 1971, but after that we went into a slumber for several decades, and air power continued to be seen as principally an instrument of warfighting.

This is where I speak about the inherent diffidence and restraint that emerged as a strategic DNA of the post-Independence Indian strategic establishment which told very heavily on the inherently offensive nature of air power. Whenever discussions on air power emerged as an instrument of coercion, the immediate refrain was that as air power is essentially escalatory, it is an instrument of warfighting, so let's leave it there. Therefore, the potential of air power in situations other than war largely went untapped, until we reached Kargil. Kargil was a full-fledged conflict, albeit a limited high intensity conflict, and gave the opportunity for air power to express itself in situations other than what India's armed forces were generally used to. But even in Kargil, I think India's use of air power was both restrained and diffident. It came in late, and therefore its full potential was not exploited. Let me amplify a little further.

Right from the beginning, the escalatory dimension of air power permeated the political establishment and the nuclear overhang seemed to delay the infusion of air power into Kargil because of the fear of the conflict expanding to other sectors or to other theatres. Now, what we didn't understand at that particular time was, what was the fear? The fear was mainly an American-led communication that cautioned against escalation because we are in a nuclear-charged environment. Now, did India really examine Pakistan's nuclear red lines; did any nuclear red lines exist across the Line of Control (LoC) in the Kargil sector? Yet Air Marshal Patney's hands were tied and the Indian Air Force was told by the political establishment: 'no crossing the Line of Control because there is a potential for escalation across fronts'. So there was a basic diffidence when it came to understanding escalation, dominance, and the role that air power can play in escalation dominance.

At the end of the day, what happened? I think air power played a significant role in de-escalation in the Kargil conflict. And nobody less than General V.P. Malik has said that had air power not come in at the time that it did, the conflict would probably have gone on for some weeks, and we would have lost another couple of hundred soldiers. I'm not saying that air power was decisive in Kargil, but it certainly enabled a quick de-escalation when it did happen.

Let me fast forward to the current environment. And before I get down to talking about limited conflict, let me argue that significant progress has been made in addressing diffidence and also in understanding the scope of air power in situations other than war. I'm glad that Lieutenant General D.S. Hooda has mentioned things like deterrence and coercion and the grey zone below conventional conflict. I think we have gradually understood that air power can play a significant role in all these genres of 'less than war scenarios'. Now, while Balakot was a good example of coercion or prevention or pre-emption using air power, the point remains: how consistent do we want to be when it comes to using air power as an instrument of coercion?

Let me take you back to 2016 to delve a little deeper into our mindsets. Admiral Arun Prakash talked about sea-blindness. I will talk about a significant lack of understanding

within not only large sections of the Indian military, but also
the Indian strategic establishment of what air power can and
cannot do. For example, and these thoughts are entirely my
own, if, and this is where I enjoy putting on a historian's hat,
in 2016, one or two of those cross-border strikes that General
Hooda orchestrated had been handed over to the Indian
Air Force, and with their targeting capability, one or two
of those targets had been taken out by the Indian Air Force
with standoff attacks, can you imagine the kind of impact it
would have had on the adversary? It would send the message
that 'we mean business'—meaning that India would use all
instruments at its disposal to coerce its western adversary.
But it took another three years for the strategic establishment
to bite the bullet of air power and exploit its full range of
coercive capabilities to impact 'less than war' situations.

Now, to limited conflict. I will depart a little bit from a
two-front strategy that General Hooda talked about, and I
will zero in further to say that with the current resources
available to the Indian Air Force, it will be very hard pressed
to deliver outcomes on an extended two-front scenario.
But when I look at a limited conflict, I would much rather
look at a single-front limited conflict but divided into
multiple sectors—maybe two or three sectors. And in such a
situation, I think the Indian Air Force has gathered significant
experience over the last couple of months to be able to put
into play full spectrum capability.

What is going to make the biggest difference in a limited
conflict is full spectrum capability. When I talk about full
spectrum capability, I want to take you back over the last few
months, from mid or end May onwards, up to the time when
the Indian Army conducted those audacious Special Forces
operations on top of the Kailash range in 2020. Please spare

a thought for what went into building up that capability—a lot of air power went into building up that capability. The Indian Air Force has never operated in such strength over eastern Ladakh. Several army officers have told me that they had never heard so many aircraft over Ladakh. If that was an expression of the direction in which the Indian Air Force is headed, and the capabilities that it has at its disposal, I think it's a step in the right direction. Because any limited conflict, whether across the Line of Actual Control (LAC) or across the LoC, will have air power as the leading element not only to hear, see and reach, but also to shape the battlefield and to cause the maximum amount of combat attrition in the shortest possible time.

We can no longer be happy with a situation along the LAC, for instance, to say that in the past we have been used to typical attrition battles. I think the days of attrition battles even along the LAC and even at those higher altitudes are gone. What the political establishment or the strategic establishment will be looking for at the end of limited high-intensity conflicts are strategic outcomes.

When you look at outcomes, there are four essential ingredients of air power that will impact phenomenally on the texture of the manner in which the conflict progresses. The first is speed and the ability to inflict shock on the adversary in a compressed timeframe. The second is the ability to provide situational awareness, both strategic and tactical, to commanders. The third is to cause heavy combat attrition beyond the range of artillery and to the extended battlefield. And the last is the ability to sustain multiple operations through the non-kinetic capabilities of air power. Now, are we assuming that a limited conflict along the LAC or along the LoC will not expand into the maritime domain?

The chances are remote, but they are not non-existent. So we must be prepared for a contingency in the maritime domain too, wherein air power, both land-based and ship-based air power, will be able to create decisive outcomes in a compressed timeframe.

Therefore, I think an understanding has crept into the military and the strategic establishment that air power should and must lead initiation of hostilities in a limited war scenario. I hope some issues of diffidence and coercion when it comes to exploitation of air power have come out clearly in this presentation.

VII

National Security Reform

Philip Campose

I will be specifically covering the subject of security reforms, which no doubt are long overdue at the national level. Although national threats and challenges are quite well defined in the Indian context, our national security apparatus appears to come up short many a time, especially when there is a major security crisis, whether it was the Chinese attacks in 1962, the Pakistani infiltrations in 1999, the Pakistan engineered 26/11 attacks in Mumbai in 2008, or the intrusions in May 2020 by China in eastern Ladakh, which is yet to be resolved fully.

It becomes obvious from such incidents that our security systems are suboptimal at places, and at times appear more geared to addressing the crises that have occurred in the past and not the ones that are likely to happen in the future. Obviously, there are shortfalls in our security systems which need to be addressed. Normally, the reforms that we undertake in the security sector are reactive and piecemeal, related to the crisis of the day. For example, the Kargil Review Committee or the Pathankot Committee and their recommendations, too, are not implemented fully and in good time.

National security reforms that India needs to undertake should result in improvements in the existing security system to the extent that, as far as possible, it should be able to predict and pre-empt all forms of security threats and challenges that the country may face in the foreseeable future. Comprehensive security reform was last attempted after the Kargil War in 1999. It may be time that even more comprehensive appraisal of India's security sector is initiated and security reforms implemented.

Security sector reforms must be at three different levels. First, reforms at the directional level, in that strategic guidance emanating from the highest authority in government should be made available to our security practitioners and possibly to the public at large.

Second, the procedural level, in that an effective and dynamic system should be made to work continuously to identify, review and proactively address national security challenges in the current and future perspective, in an efficient and foolproof manner.

And third, the execution level, where the military, paramilitary, police, cyber, and intelligence agencies should be continually strengthened, optimally structured and resourced in terms of tasking, training, equipment and budget support to carry out their role and tasks in a more effective manner, which precludes getting caught off guard or ill-equipped whenever the next crisis takes place.

Let us now look at the reforms required at these three levels of national security one by one. Let me start with the directional level. What has been missing so far is strategic guidance in the security realm that the government of the day must articulate clearly and provide to the security practitioners. The best way to do that is to enunciate a national security strategy for the country, say for a five-year period. And for an emerging power of India's strengths and resources, which seeks developed-country status economically and the global rule-maker status politically, the national security strategy should predominantly reflect our hopes, rather than our fears. In that, it is our aspiration for a leadership role in the global committee of nations that should primarily guide us in formulating our strategy, rather than just addressing our security concerns.

No doubt our security system should display foresight, alertness and strength in terms of an effective intelligence and police capacity, backed by a strong military deterrence capability and internal security reserves, which we are able to operationalize at short notice to deal with any threat that manifests on our borders or within. But it is equally important that from that position of strength we are successful in creating a peaceful security environment, both within the country and on our borders, which would contribute to rapid economic growth and the people enjoying the fruits of resultant prosperity, as was mentioned by Ambassador Chinoy.

Clearly, an emerging power of India's stature and potential should not be satisfied with an eternally unstable situation on any of our borders or within. We should treat such episodes only as temporary hiccups or setbacks, meant to be resolved, so that stability is restored at the earliest. Strangely, all this while the primary focus of our defence forces and other security means has remained on Pakistan, the weaker of our adversaries. There should be no doubts left: the events in eastern Ladakh over the last year have given a clear message that it is time to shift our primary focus to China, a stronger adversary, which continues to display a confrontational stance, both politically and militarily.

Our national security strategy must give a clear message highlighting adherence to our traditional values of democracy, equality, freedom, and pluralism, which have gained us an enduring place in the hearts and minds of the global community, a positive image as a country and a people, which distinguishes us clearly from the authoritarian, aggressive and hegemonic nations which do not provide the fruits of these enduring values to their people. The national security strategy should also cover the non-traditional aspects of security, like water, energy, environment, pandemic, and financial network security, all of which are very important for the sense of well-being among the people of our country.

Next, the procedural level. We are aware that in our parliamentary system, the highest decision-making body on security matters is the Cabinet Committee on Security. The cabinet ministers who form this committee control the resources and means that provide security to the country. Further, the parliamentary standing committees associated with these ministries provide legislative oversight to ensure efficient functioning of these ministries. This is a system which needs enhancement in a number of ways.

In parallel we have a system where the national security adviser, with support from the National Security Council (NSC) and the National Security Advisory Board, provide advice on security matters to the PMO (Prime Minister's Office). Both these systems should not be seen to be functioning independent of each other. We need to strengthen these institutions and optimize the output of and coordination between the ministries, agencies and the

NSC. Otherwise, there will be gaps which will be exploited, especially by our adversaries.

Various subsystems in our security system must be put through periodic review, in keeping with developments in the security environment and improvements in the technological means available to us. And timely action must be taken on the recommendations of these committees without waiting for the next crisis to happen.

And finally, the execution level. I'm sure we all agree on the need for capacity building of our security forces, who provide the means to execute our security plans and measures. The most important reform would entail strengthening and modernizing our military, police, paramilitary, cyber and intelligence agencies and structures, as well as improving the coordination between them. As far as possible, such measures should not result in increasing the number of personnel in these forces. This would require articulation of a National Defence Strategy, increase in defence budget until our defence modernization needs are achieved, restructuring the forces by improving the quality of our military units and technology while cutting down on quantities, including number of personnel. Raising of the Mountain Strike Corps and other related accretions in the form originally envisaged would need to be completed, if not done so already. Rebalancing our forces between the various fronts may be opportune at this juncture.

Our strategic forces would need to be further strengthened and modernized. Our nuclear doctrine may need a review. The operational functioning of the military, paramilitary and police forces must be optimized by integrating resources and removing duplication of effort. Appointment of the Chief of Defence Staff (CDS) as of last year is an important step in this direction. However, a lot more needs to be done in terms of achieving genuine integration and optimization of effort. The theatre commands will have to be put into effect at the earliest. Air defence and logistics of the three services need to be integrated.

The procurement system needs total revamping, a more efficient and cost-effective system needs to be put in place to provide the best bang for the buck. And that too in a timely manner. Correct prioritization of our competing needs holds the key. Efforts at self-reliance definitely need to take off, but not at the cost of the efficiency and the effectiveness of our forces, which would happen in case the products are unreliable. The functioning of the Defence Research and Development Organization (DRDO) and Defence Public Sector Undertakings (DPSUs) need further review and optimization as part of this process.

To sum up, I believe that the recent tensions with China have provided us an opportunity to review our national security challenges and put much needed security reforms into effect. I would also like to reiterate that a well thought out national security strategy needs to be enunciated at the earliest, following which a comprehensive strategic review of the effectiveness of our national security architecture and systems should be done and reforms put in place. The faster this is done, the sooner would we be confident of effectively handling our security challenges of the future in the best way possible.

VIII

India's National Security Challenges
Centre–State Responsibilities

C. Uday Bhaskar

I would like to begin by recognizing that many among the participants at this webinar have a deeper water table than me apropos national security. My perch is that of an analyst who is still studying the subject and making notes.

The trigger for this talk is a series of conversations that one had over the last two years with members of the IIC regarding national security, following which Mr N.N. Vohra, President IIC, convened a few informal meetings with domain experts and heads of think tanks. I had suggested at the time that the membership of the IIC represented a very rich but untapped gene pool of expertise and experience in matters of national security and many have been practitioners and policymakers of rare pedigree. Mr Vohra is a case in point as he has the unique distinction of having been both Defence Secretary and Home Secretary at the centre, as also Principal Secretary to the Prime Minister and Governor of the troubled (erstwhile) state of J&K for an extended period.

There has been a fair amount of churning with respect to national security in recent years since Kargil 1999, and some useful reports, documents and books are now available in the public domain. While these are useful in irrigating a vital issue, alas they have not resulted in the kind of institutional redress that is required. Hence, from Kargil 1999, Mumbai 2008 to Galwan 2020, lessons remain to be learnt and correctives applied.

What I have to say will be relatively familiar and the objective of my talk is more to stimulate a set of similar deliberations that will enable a pooling of national security know-how and domain-specific expertise that can be shaped into policy relevant inputs. And I believe the IIC and its members could play a valuable role in this endeavour.

National security is both an old chestnut and a complex domain as far as public policy issues go, and has been reviewed and discussed periodically in different fora. I use the term 'old chestnut' since I recall that this was my introduction to the IIC Round Tables many years ago when these matters were deliberated upon. This was the period when Mr John Lal and Mr Uma Shankar Bajpai were at the helm.

The reason I characterize the concept of national security as a complex domain is because of its DNA, which is inclusive, expansive, multi-tiered and opaque. We are still waiting for the Henderson Brooks–Bhagat Report relating to the 1962 debacle to be placed in the public domain.

The concept of national security has an anomalous quality, in that it has certain constant elements that relate to both the entity of the state and the citizen. The sanctity of national sovereignty and the pursuit of human well-being are illustrative. National security also has a dynamic quality, wherein significant transmutations take place due to the impact of technology, and therefore we refer to techno-strategic imbrications: that is, the synergy between technology and strategy.

In the twentieth century the shift from the horse to the tank or the arrival of radar and sonar are illustrative at one level, while the advent of the apocalyptic atomic age as represented by Hiroshima and Nagasaki in August 1945 marked the emergence of weapons of mass destruction (WMD) into the national security calculus.

It is against this backdrop that I wish to dwell briefly on the first part of my talk, namely 'India's National Security Challenges'. I'm cognizant of the grim reality that today's deliberation is taking place when India is grappling with the COVID-19 pandemic which is an unprecedented public health crisis that has severely impacted human security in a stark and stressing manner.

In relation to the challenges of national security that India is facing, the first bullet, a familiar one, is to acknowledge that national security can no longer be prioritized in an exclusive manner and much less in terms of hard security or the military dimension alone. The anomalous end of the Cold War testified to the tenet that national security in today's context is an inclusive concept, and one way to visualize it is in the form of a hexagon wherein the primary strands are the political, economic and military attributes.

Complementing these are the technological, environmental and human security determinants. This distillate has also been referred to as comprehensive national capability or power, and finding the appropriate equipoise along all the six elements is a perennial challenge for the policymaker and national leadership.

The related second bullet apropos this inclusive definition of national security is that the state has to acquire both the capacity and the competence to anticipate, to the extent possible, and manage the challenge before it morphs into a threat and finally a crisis. To cite recent examples, both the Galwan crisis of 2020 and the current COVID-19 surge are illustrative of how security exigencies can spiral out of control.

This brings me to the next link in this lattice—namely that the pursuit of national security in the twenty-first century has to foreground the well-being of the citizen in an equitable and empathetic manner by those who have been entrusted with the mandate to govern.

This is not new as a formulation, and many will recall the Arthashastra, wherein Kautilya, the emperor of ancient times, was exhorted to ensure the *yogakshema* or well-being of the citizen. The current pandemic has highlighted the lack of appropriate capacity in relation to public health infrastructure, and any future review of resource allocation will have to factor in human security in a composite and empathetic manner.

Thus, when it comes to the spectrum of national security, it is to envisage it in a holistic and inclusive manner beginning with the territorial integrity of the geography of India in its entirety—from Kashmir to Kanyakumari, and from the Andaman and Nicobar islands to Lakshadweep-Minicoy—and concurrently ensure that human security and well-being—the *yogakshema*—of this vast demography of 1.4 billion is not compromised or transgressed inadvertently or deliberately.

This is a daunting task for those who have been entrusted with the pursuit and protection or distribution of this composite security, which is why one may aver that national security responsibility, or *dayatva*, is a 24/7 treadmill.

Let me turn now to centre–state responsibilities in relation to national security. As pointed out by experts, under the Indian Constitution national security is not a subject specifically listed in any of the three lists, that is, the Union, the State or the Concurrent List.

Under Part XVIII, Articles 352 and 355 refer to external aggression and internal disturbance and the role of the Union government. In a normative sense, it stands to reason that both centre and state have a shared responsibility when it comes to national security and ought to be on the same page, particularly in relation to the external domain.

The broad principle that obtains in relation to governance and policy is that 'security' in a macro sense and along the external contour of the country is a responsibility that devolves on the centre in Delhi, and that law and order is a state subject—meaning that chief ministers of states and lieutenant governors in the case of union territories—have the responsibility to maintain 'law and order' which has a direct bearing on the well-being of the citizen.

Given the complex diversity and nature of India's socio-political trajectory from August 1947, centre-state political discord and dissonance is as old as the Republic. The imposition of President's Rule by the centre in individual states for a perceived breakdown in law and order and other transgressions as perceived by the centre and the concerned state are part of the Indian historical narrative and have continued from Nehru to Modi. The need to review what was envisioned by the founding fathers against the actual unspooling of Indian politics led to the Justice Puncchi Report that was submitted to the government in March 2010, which is an exhaustive document in seven volumes with 273 recommendations.

However, in the last decade there has not been any evidence to suggest that the more substantive recommendations to reduce centre-state discord in matters relating to internal security and law and order have been internalized by both interlocutors. The aftermath of the 26/11 terror attack in Mumbai 2008 and the acrimony over the National Investigation Agency (NIA) et al. are cases in point. And recall that leading the charge at the time to protect the rights of state governments in relation to law and order was the then Chief Minister of Gujarat Narendra Modi, who is now the Prime Minister.

While the current political orientation in the country may not be conducive to a radical improvement in centre-state amity due to deep ideological divergences between the Bharatiya Janata Party (BJP) and some of its principal opponents, two areas merit scrutiny for their long-term national security implications.

The first relates to the external domain. Two incidents are illustrative. The imprudently conceived and executed Indian Peace Keeping Force (IPKF) effort in Sri Lanka and the more recent Mizoram–Myanmar refugee issue are illustrative. Separated by almost 30 years, the Delhi–Chennai dissonance over the LTTE was a tragic case wherein the political contestation within Tamil Nadu was detrimental to the objectives being pursued by Delhi, the result of which was a tragic loss of lives and, I would add, Indian credibility.

In March 2021, the Mizoram Chief Minister Mr Zoramthangma conveyed his views on the Chin refugees and their affinity with the local tribes in Mizoram. In public comments he added: 'It may be mentioned that the Myanmar areas bordering Mizoram are inhabited by Chin communities who are ethnically our Mizo brethren with whom we have been having close contacts throughout all these years even before India became independent.'

The Aizawl–Delhi differences over the policies to be adopted in relation to the civil war in Myanmar resulted in a tense fortnight with instructions from the state government being overruled by Delhi. This airing of such differences over a matter that has grave security and policy implications in the public domain was avoidable, but it was allowed to play out in front of the cameras.

The second area of centre–state discord relates to law and order and the manner in which electoral politics and a deep-seated inter-party power struggle have led to a very serious distortion of existing protocols and practices. Two unsavoury incidents are indicative of what lies ahead, alas. The Mumbai Police Commissioner incident and the current Central Bureau of Investigation (CBI) arrest of Trinamool Congress members in West Bengal have attracted adverse comments for the selective interpretation of the law and the manner in which central agencies have been tasked.

As an analyst, my reading is that unless there is effective and objective judicial intervention in such matters—the centre-state discord on sensitive security related issues—as also in matters pertaining to law and order with a political overhang will deteriorate in the years ahead. This augurs poorly for the texture of India's composite national security.

Let me now turn to what sates can perhaps do as part of their own contribution to the national security discourse. The first observation is that every state and union territory in India has its own security experience and a set of issues that it needs to prioritize. In other words, Maharashtra,

Chattisgarh and Mizoram have different security challenges and hence capabilities would have to be acquired accordingly.

The Puncchi Report provides a useful starting point and each state could embark upon a review of its own security challenges and the harmonization with the 2010 report. To this end, the creation of a state perspective planning cell with professionals drawn from local human resources like the state government, academia and think tanks/civil society could be encouraged. A state-specific security ecosystem would slowly grow and the recommendations of such a group could provide the substance for further review and allocation of resources.

In the earlier part of my talk I made reference to technology and its impact on the prosperity and security of the state and the citizen. The twenty-first century will be one where the most intense contestations and animation are likely to take place in the maritime–cyberspace continuum. AI, robotics, spectrum dominance and more will be the new tools of state power and corporate tech giants.

How is this relevant to the average Indian state and what is the co-relation with national security? My focus is on the cyber domain. Globalization and the current digitally driven economic–trade patterns are heavily dependent on cyber capabilities. Many experts aver that the major security challenge India has to be prepared for is cyber attacks, big and small. As per NCRB data, the total number of cyber crimes reported in 2010 was 1,322 and this increased to 44,546 in 2019; and this may well be the tip of the iceberg.

While India is investing in cyber capabilities at the central level, there is to my mind a strong case for individual states to invest in nurturing cyber skills. This in turn leads to education and the creation of infrastructure, wherein the private sector in individual states could be prevailed upon to become stakeholders for the economic-trade linkages need little reiteration.

The multi-layered nature of the inclusive security paradigm is evident when we see this exploration leading to the need to recognize the centrality of education, again a state subject. India's younger demography, the human resource that must be equipped to engage with the challenges and opportunities of a 5G world, has to become far more proficient in acquiring a scientific temperament and understand the need to value rigorous education in mathematics and the sciences.

Recent reports that the average Indian student could shed mathematics at Class 10 and yet seek higher education in engineering and other science-related disciplines was baffling. One hopes this is not policy cast in stone.

India's external and internal security have become interlinked and overlap in areas like state sponsored terrorism and cyber crimes. The possibility of unmanned drones and underwater submersibles posing serious security challenges in the near future is a high probability. The cyber-underwater cable linkage needs little reiteration. While the centre in Delhi will continue to have the primary responsibility for national security, individual states can make a significant contribution in specific niches. Bringing security onto the state radar in an informed and holistic manner could be a first step.

One hopes that the IIC can provide a platform to enable such deliberations to improve our collective understanding of India's national security challenges.

What is dismaying to me as an analyst is the ostrich act that India remains committed to when it comes to national security. This is a subject that is rarely deliberated upon in parliament in an informed, objective and non-partisan manner. The Khanduri Report was the last parliamentary defence committee report that was substantive and has met the same fate as the 2000 Kargil review: lip service. While the current pandemic-induced resource constraints are to be acknowledged, there are many inadequacies that need to be redressed apropos the management of India's composite national security. Centre-state relations and responsibilities is one strand. I hope my remarks will stimulate more deliberations on this vital subject.

IX

Higher Defence Management Reforms
Some Challenges

Srinjoy Chowdhury

W orking in discrete silos, two intelligence-gathering units of the Indian Army and the Indian Air Force flew camera-mounted Unmanned Aerial Vehicles or UAVs out of the Jammu airbase. When the images arrived, the units remained distant neighbours, former Northern Army Commander Lieutenant General D.S. Hooda (Retd) remembered; they chose not to share the images with each other. Is this the best way of fighting and winning the next war? In this era of jointness, certainly not, not when modern warfare demands that India's armed forces plan together, train together and fight together. There's growing consensus about the need for change, but there's very little unanimity about much else.

The former Northern Army commander's Jammu story isn't a one-off; there are other examples of the Army, Navy and the Air Force having had separate objectives, separate plans.

*A summary of the discussions held among the panelists, prepared by Srinjoy Chowdhury.

'Each service has its own communication infrastructure, and we don't talk among each other—the Army communication network cannot talk directly to the Air Force Communication network or the Naval communication network,' Lieutenant General Hooda (Retd) regretted. It's another reminder that in this era of cyber insecurity and information warfare, when 'there are no boundaries between civil and military,' it is imperative for the armed forces to 'integrate'. At the IIC's webinar, moderated by Lieutenant General Satish Dua (Retd), former Chief of Integrated Defence Staff, Lieutenant General Hooda (Retd) and two former chiefs, Admiral Arun Prakash (Retd) and Air Chief Marshal Fali Major (Retd), agreed to disagree about how India's national security apparatus needs restructuring.

Beginning the discussions, Lieutenant General Dua (Retd) noted that India began well, and right after Independence too, recognizing the need for the armed forces to work together: the National Defence Academy (NDA) for cadets was tri-service as were the Defence Services Staff College in Ooty for middle-level officers and the National Defence College in Delhi. That's where it ended, and now, seven decades after Independence has begun a serious stab at integration with the appointment of the Chief of Defence Staff (CDS), first suggested after the Kargil War, in 1999 and under him, the creation of the Department of Military Affairs (DMA). There is talk of theatre commands, with each theatre commander having Army, Navy and Air Force personnel and weaponry under his command, and in complete charge of operations in that geographical zone. In the future, the chiefs of staff, who are currently responsible for warfare, could only be left with recruitment and training of personnel and providing armaments to the theatre commands. It also means sharing available resources, and a division of assets, tasks that are seldom easy and inevitably controversial. Before the big decisions, the changes that will restructure the armed forces into a twenty-first century war-machine, lean, mean and technologically top-of-the-line, several issues, Lieutenant General Dua (Retd) felt, needed to be clarified.

First, with the appointment of the CDS and the decision to form integrated theatre commands (four in all—the army-led Western and Northern Commands, presumably to handle Pakistan and China respectively, an Indian Air Force-led Air Defence Command and a Navy-led Peninsular Command [this includes all of central and southern India and the island territories]), who will take the decisions? Also, isn't there a need to change the way the political leadership, the bureaucracy and the armed forces interact with each other? What then, is the ideal civil-military decision-making structure during war and peace?

Second, even before the restructuring is attempted, is there need for a new doctrine, a National Defence Doctrine or a National Security Doctrine?

And finally, the Indian Air Force's reservations about the current restructuring. How can they be resolved?

These are not Gordian knots that need an Alexander of Macedon, but they're complex issues that have, so far, eluded consensus. Here, four senior commanders, 14 stars between them, have attempted to find appropriate, and importantly, acceptable solutions.

THEATRE COMMANDS

For years and years, India paid 'lip service' to the idea of commands, without really understanding the 'actual implications of jointness,' Admiral Prakash (Retd) began. Over the years, he said, the armed forces 'failed to achieve jointness in training, in operations, in planning… While we learnt a few lessons when we achieved success in campaigns or battles, it was more in the nature of good fortune.' Then came the 'jolt' of the Kargil war and the 'jolt' produced the joint Andamans and Nicobar Command and the Strategic Forces Command (SFC), which controls India's nuclear weapons. Calling the appointment of the CDS and the creation of the DMA within the Ministry of Defence (MoD) 'bold' steps, he regretted he had never heard of the term theaterization, earlier and nor is it 'in any dictionary'. It has not, he said, taken India 'in the right direction'. Why have theatre commands before the armed forces are properly integrated? Why talk of theatres before the structures, procedures and processes are firmly in place? 'By using the term "theaterization" at the beginning, within days or weeks of the formation of the Department of Military Affairs, people started talking about theatre commands which are… not clearly understood. I do believe our focus should be on jointness,' he added.

Referring to the first CDS, the late Bipin Rawat's statement about the Air Force (he had said it was a 'support arm'), Admiral Prakash (Retd) said air power 'has been an issue of contention' all over the world, with different countries having different solutions. 'It is time we recognize air power as an element, not the IAF. Air power is an issue because it is wielded by the other services… but the IAF has a broad proprietary sense about air power. The chiefs need to trash this out.'

Every country, he said, has had to wrestle with the integration problem. India needs a suitable solution and India needs to see what other countries have done, and even learn from their mistakes. Refuting charges that the Andaman and Nicobar Command, the first tri-service effort and now 20 years old, was a failure; it was, he said, a 'great success for the purpose for which it was created—the principle of best joint venture and jointness. It was not replicated, it was neglected and therefore labelled a failure. Let us learn from others' mistakes, let us not dodge difficult questions, let us sit down at the table.' Admiral Prakash's final thrust at theatre commands was that there should be 'no rush... until and unless we have complete agreement.' Nor did the government want theatre commands within three years of the CDS' appointment: it was only to 'bring in jointness in operations, logistics...'.

If you have to have theatre commands, he said, 'the war-fighting functions should involve only combatant commanders (of the theatres) in New Delhi where at present the chiefs are performing the fighting and staff functions.' Also, the number of commands, currently all of 17, must come down to four or five.

Almost dismissive about the theatre commands as they are being talked about today, Air Chief Marshal Major (Retd) began with an admission: he couldn't 'understand the proposal to have land theatres, maritime theatres and (an) air defence command. The very concept and meaning of an integrated theatre command is lost when one particular service is designated primary. This is the main bone of contention.'

The former Air Force chief had different views about how a theatre command, assuming there was one, would function, it 'should be a true joint tri-service command with the theatre commander a person rotated among the three services with qualified component commanders from the other services also.' The former Air Chief Marshal's idea of jointness envisages an army officer, for example, heading the peninsular command and a navy or Air Force officer in charge of the western or northern commands. Any theatre command should be 'geographic and threat-centric; it does not mean one air defence command, one maritime command, and the rest as land commands.' And importantly, 'all three services have a role to play.'

'Instead of creating theatre commands, there should be only one to start with as a test bed: northern command, where all the fighting has taken place,' he said, speaking of the 1971 Kargil War and the ongoing problem in east Ladakh. 'If we set up a theatre command there, the true jointness amongst all the services will be realized.... We should not be in a hurry to form a theatre command,' he added.

Agreeing with Air Chief Marshal Major (Retd) about 'rotational' appointments (meaning that commanders of all three services could head all the commands—an Air Force or Navy officer heading the northern and western commands or an army officer heading the peninsular or air defence commands), Lieutenant General Dua explained he was in principle, agreed, but it would take time to have sufficiently senior 'purple' (an armed forces officer sufficiently 'integrated' and having necessary understanding about other services or simply, a colour signifying the satisfactory integration of the Army's olive-green, the Navy's white and Air Force's blue) personnel. Two prospective theatre commands, he argued (west and north) were adversary centric.

Lieutenant General Hooda (Retd) noted that the current 'war-fighting model' is 'fairly service specific' and 'not conducive' to joint operations, even the command structures in the armed forces are not right. 'There is hardly any joint planning as every service makes its own war plans. Therefore, there is a need to bring in a level of integration and jointness in war-fighting for which one may need certain structures.... The larger issue is what should be the process of creating these?' Like Admiral Prakash (Retd) and Air Chief Marshal Major (Retd) before him, he felt it was important 'not to be in too much of a hurry' to create theatre commands. What is imperative is a joint war-fighting doctrine. Without one, 'we do not even have a national security strategy... How are we going to make our plans?... And this joint war-fighting doctrine will also cover issues like the best employment of air power.'

His prescription is joint 'professional military education', a doctrine, of course and then, 'greater integration at the lower levels. Once all this is in place, 'should we not then think of putting up an integrated theatre command... this approach may be better than creating integrated theatres first and then concentrating on everything else.'

Agreeing with Air Chief Marshal Major (Retd), where he has served and where there's fighting virtually every day, he felt that Northern Command ought to be a test bed. He wondered if the Central Armed Police Forces (CAPF) in Jammu and Kashmir and also, Ladakh like the Central Reserve Police Forces (CRPF), the Border Security Force (BSF) and the Indo-Tibetan Border Police (ITBP) would also be part of the integration process as also, the Air Force.

Lieutenant General Dua (Retd) pointed out that 'putting out doctrines is hard' as 'it is difficult to get the three services to come to evolve and write doctrines.' It would mean goalposts being changed during the presumably spirited discussions and therefore, a delay in creating the theatre commands. But Northern Command as a test bed, he agreed, would be a good idea.

CHAIN OF COMMAND

With the appointment of the CDS, there's a new chain of command; it's also time, said Admiral Prakash (Retd) for the *Raksha Mantri* (Defence Minister) to 'dirty his hands and actually look after national security and defence, which so far no Defence Minister has done. That's in peacetime. In wartime, it is the Prime Minister who gives the overall directions (about) how the war should be conducted.' For, the CDS has (right now) no operational authority, he noted, but is the senior-most armed forces officer and the principal military advisor to the Defence Minister.

Different countries have different systems. In the United States, it is the head of state—the President who directs the Defence Minister (called Defence Secretary), who interacts with the combatant commanders. In Britain, there's a CDS reporting to the Defence Minister (also called Defence Secretary) and then the Prime Minister. India has to 'evolve a new paradigm,' putting 'the PM wholly in the picture.' The *Raksha Mantri* will have the advice of the CDS readily available to him, both for strategic planning and conducting operations in times of war. Sadly, the defence ministers he worked with were 'intelligent and intellectually accomplished, but as our politicians are so engrossed in politics, elections, etc., they had no time for defence or national security. We have to find a way to relieve our defence ministers of other preoccupations so that they can actually get involved in matters of defence and national security,' declared Admiral Prakash (Retd).

India, the Admiral regretted, must 'be the only major power in the world which has not issued a defence white paper on national security and it's time for the Government of India to do so. At present, we are operating in a vacuum.' Once there is one, the *Raksha Mantri* can issue the necessary directives and importantly, provide the necessary funds.

Like Admiral Prakash (Retd), Lieutenant General Hooda (Retd) too felt the *Raksha Mantri* needs 'to get much more involved in operational issues. We keep returning to the argument that there is a lack of political objectives for military planning, but we are not completely clear as to what the political aim is. As we look forward to our future war-fighting models, I think it's important that the political leadership gets much more involved.'

And what of the CDS? He's out of the operational loop right now, but once the theatre commands are ready, 'he will have to be somewhere in the operational chain,' pointed out Lieutenant General Hooda (Retd). In any case, he is part of the recently created agencies dealing with cyber warfare, space and the special forces, which could be joint commands in the future. Where, then, do the three chiefs fit in? 'If the chain of command is from the theatre commanders to the CDS, then the chiefs will have only a limited role in terms of planning?' he asked. What responsibilities will they have? Who will allocate resources to the theatres? 'This needs more discussion, but the bottom line is that political leadership needs to get more involved in defence planning.'

For Air Chief Marshal Major (Retd), there are far too many unanswered questions. Will the theatre commanders be 3-star generals or 4-star? If they are 4-star, they will report directly to the political leadership, but if they are lieutenant generals, a rung below (which is very likely) would they report to the CDS, making him double-hatted? 'He is the single-point advisor to the government and also becomes the commander-in-chief. Is that desirable?' In the United States, he added, the Chairman, Joint Chiefs of Staff, is prohibited, by law, from taking any operational decisions as he is the single-point advisor to the political leadership. If the theatre commander is four-star and reporting directly to the government, where does that leave the Defence Secretary (the senior-most civilian in the ministry, who according to the rules of business of the Government of India, responsible for the country's security)? 'With the newly-created Department of Military Affairs (DMA) looking after major HR issues like promotions and postings, the retired air chief marshal regretted the absence of civilian oversight in these matters. It would serve the forces better,' he added.

In the new era, with operational work the theatre commands' responsibility, all the chiefs will have to do is 'train, sustain and equip,' something the Air Force is not comfortable with, he said. Moving a squadron of fighter aircraft from say, the east to the north during conflict, it is done 'seamlessly'. Air force resources are allotted to a certain sector, 'can be pulled out at any time. If you move a brigade to the north, pulling that brigade out will take a month of Sundays. These are issues we have to think about' before any decision is made about the chain of command.

Agreeing with Air Chief Marshal Major (Retd) about moving air force units, Lieutenant General Dua (Retd) pointed out that the American system works on both 'forces on allocation and forces on allotment, meaning that a command already has forces and depending on the situation, could get more from a central reserve. Referring to the Defence Secretary's status after the restructuring, things have to change, with an amendment, if necessary. The government, he said, according to the rules of business 1961, functions through ministries, headed by a minister and below him, department heads, usually secretaries. As the Army, Navy and Air Force were not departments, the Defence Secretary headed the defence department. Now, with the creation of the DMA, things would naturally change, he argued.

CIVIL-MILITARY RELATIONS

Along with jointness, there has to be 'civil-military integration, which we have not managed to achieve in 50–70 years,' said Admiral Arun Prakash (Retd), with the MoD manned entirely by civilians and the service HQ by uniformed people 'who only spoke to each other on files.' While a man in uniform is a secretary in the MoD (the CDS heading the DMA), for the first time since Independence, he wondered how well it will work. 'I'm not sure how many people from the IAS are happy to serve in the department of military affairs. I was part of the Naresh Chandra Committee where it was clearly stated that no IAS personnel would like to serve under a military person… If that be the case, we need to create a new cadre of national security civil servants drawn from the civil services who are willing and happy to serve in the ministries of foreign affairs, defence and home affairs.' If civil servants are still reluctant to integrate with the military, 'I am not sure how successful our new reform is going to be,' he added.

One way of avoiding friction and ensuring 'more willing integration,' Admiral Prakash (Retd) felt, is by ensuring the Defence Secretary and the CDS have the same status. 'If we look at the British and Australian patterns, the Defence Secretary has been raised to the level of the Chief of Defence

Staff. Then, in India, the Defence Secretary can attend the Chief of Staff Committee meetings and the CDS be present at the Defence Secretary's'.

The fly in the ointment remains, Admiral Prakash (Retd.) said, with the Government of India's rules of business, recently amended, continuing to have the Defence Secretary as responsible for the defence of India and additionally, for defence planning. 'I'm not sure why this happened because this was the time to do things right... These issues need to be faced if the DMA is actually going to be a significant change. Otherwise, it will consist of uniformed people running around in circles as we have done for 70 years. We need people from the IAS and the Indian Defence Accounts Services to actually work wholly and royally in the DMA.'

Things weren't so bleak any more, assured Lieutenant General Dua (Retd). Among the DMA staff were 20 civilian officers—1 additional secretary, 6 joint secretaries and 13 undersecretaries, but there's room for improvement, he acknowledged: the Ministry of External Affairs officials don't like moving to the Defence Ministry, but things have to improve. 'If the government can take the bold step to appoint the CDS, surely, today or tomorrow, it will happen.'

- Agreeing with Admiral Prakash (Retd) about where civil-military relations in India stood, Air Chief Marshal Major (Retd) pointed out that it was often about personalities. 'If any important file needed to be moved by Air HQ, the Defence Secretary was extremely accommodating because of the urgency. This doesn't always happen.' Speaking about how armed forces personnel and civilians work together in the newly created DMA, where additional and joint secretaries are posted, he felt that 'merely posting a person there is not going to help.' The retired air chief wondered if there's sufficient 'give-and-take between them'. Integration would happen, he said, when there's 'jointness with the civilians'. And jointness isn't just the Army, Navy and Air Force working together, he added, remembering his efforts to amend the Union War Book. 'I was amazed to see absolutely archaic systems that belonged to the 1940s or 1950s. I took it upon myself to amend the Union War Book which is a gargantuan task because every single ministry is involved. When you talk of civil-military relations and coordination, I found that for eight months I was there, not a thing had happened, but we pressed on... I came to know it was amended in 2013.' Coordination, he said, is not just about soldiers and civilians working together in the DMA, but a larger effort, a government approach involving the MoD and the Ministry of External Affairs, and also, everyone who matters needs to sit down to discuss the issues. Only then can there be a national security strategy, not just by getting the armed forces to work together.

- A joint forces doctrine already exists, pointed out Lieutenant General Dua (Retd). It's also in the public domain. Putting it together was impossibly difficult. He spoke of the 'great friction' and the 'consultations which were very difficult to obtain.' But it's there and in the absence of something more substantial, it's something to work with.

Speaking about decision making at the highest level, Lieutenant General Hooda (Retd) said the National Security Council, headed by the Prime Minister, with senior ministers in support and the National Security Advisor (NSA) providing secretarial services, does exist. There's also the Strategic Policy Group comprising top bureaucrats and also, the chiefs of the armed forces, but no political leaders. And under that there's the National Security Advisory Board, a group of retired people. 'There is no real formal architecture or organizational structure where, on a regular basis, the political leadership, the military leadership and other organs of government, particularly foreign policy experts, can all sit together. I think that is where the big deficiency is.'

When Lieutenant General Dua (Retd) pointed out that the recently created Defence Planning Committee, where the defence, finance and external affairs ministries can work together is 'a very small substitute' and 'several functional issues' were sorted out, Lieutenant General Hooda (Retd) replied that it has 'further removed the service chiefs from access to the Defence Minister.' It has its advantages, he acknowledged, as 'it brings together other ministries, but I still think that the direct advice has been further distanced.'

AIR POWER

One of the four theatre commands being envisaged deals with air defence. This is something, said Air Chief Marshal Major (Retd), the Air Force had never proposed. Air defence, he added, is a '24/7, 365-day task of the IAF, irrespective of peace and war. There are over 7,500 aircraft... crisscrossing the Indian skies on a daily basis and it is the job of the IAF, in conjunction with the civil surveillance and other radars which are available in the country, to make sure there are no intrusions. Air defence is monitoring, picking up, tracking and if necessary, intercepting hostile aircraft'. The IAF has been doing this for decades as the 'radars, the sensors, the guided weapon squadrons' are 'carefully and strategically' placed.

There are no aircraft exclusively for air defence. All of them can be used for ground attack, air superiority or air defence, and even reconnaissance. 'It's just a matter of changing roles. This is the IAF's biggest issue: the scarce resources available are already very well placed in both peacetime and forward locations... if theatre commands with a geographic orientation are forced, there will be no problem because the resources can be used in those areas. But if we talk of an Air Defence Command, what role will they (the warplanes) have? They are doing what they do on a daily basis anyway. If the Army's and Navy's shore-based air defence assets have to be part of the Air Defence Command, there is a need to have secure communications and data links. They aren't there as yet.'

The Air Defence Commander is a theatre commander, but even now there are major-general level air defence chiefs in every command. 'So, what is new?' he asked. Besides, there's a need to look at what other countries have done with their Air Defence Commands. 'Many advanced countries like Russia and the USA created Air Defence Commands and disbanded them because they were not working out. For any air defence operation, real time situational awareness is very, very essential.'

The retired air chief went even further. 'Why Air Defence Command? If the service which is going to undertake this task has not mooted this idea, I wonder where it has come from. That, in today's context, is a bone of contention between the IAF and the Army.' As for the Navy, the Air Force provides air defence up to India's Special Economic Zone, he added. 'After that, the Navy has its own air defence.' It is not clear, he lamented, what 'the reason for creating an Air Defence Command' actually is.

If there's been no consultation before talking of an Air Defence Command, there's 'no logic' behind creating the

Peninsular Command, declared Admiral Prakash (Retd). The announcements about the theatre commands were made right after the DMA was created, evidence of preconceived ideas and the lack of proper consultation. 'Air power has been an issue of contention not only in India, but in other parts of the world. But they have found ways to get around it. The IAF has been quite insecure about placing its assets under the command of any other service and they have a good reason for it. In the 1970s, there was a long drawn and rather ugly battle for control of maritime reconnaissance between the Navy and the IAF. Eventually, the government decided to give the role to the Navy. Ten years later, in 1986, the Army fought for and created an Army Air Corps, which also took some assets from the IAF. At that time, there was a fight over combat helicopters. The Defence Ministry has not taken (these differences) into account.'

The Air Force, he felt, is worried about its 'assets', being controlled by others. And that will do harm to the service. 'I think, to an extent, they are justified in their fears.' There's also a difference between the way the Air Force sees how air power has to be used (its 2012 doctrine speaks of acquiring strategic reach and capabilities across the spectrum of conflict), and how the other services see it (something to be used to attain objectives). 'The very fact that the Chief of Defence Staff (then Bipin Rawat, who died in a helicopter crash on 8 December 2021) said the IAF is a supporting arm shows he had something in mind.'

Now that the issue is in the open, Admiral Prakash (Retd) said, the role of the Air Force can 'only be decided if the three chiefs agree to sit down, perhaps with an umpire to make sure it happens now. We don't want to copy other countries, but that is exactly what happened in the USA in 1947. They passed the National Security Act and created the US Air Force. A fight broke out about air power between the three services almost immediately. James Forrestal, the Defence Secretary (the Indian equivalent of the Defence Minister) took the chiefs to Key West in Florida, secured them in a cabin for the weekend till they came up with an agreement. The Key West agreement decided (what) role air power had to play in the Army, Navy and Air Force. We must take this opportunity to decide the roles, missions, the competencies and who is to do what as far as air power is concerned.' Otherwise, he warned, 'this sniping will carry on even after we've created theatre commands.'

Agreeing with both Air Chief Marshal Major (Retd) and Admiral Prakash (Retd), Lieutenant General Hooda (Retd) said it was important for the CDS and the three chiefs to sit down and 'discuss and debate' the air power issue. If a proper joint war-fighting doctrine were in place, 'how airpower is going to be employed, worries about whether it could be misused or mishandled… a lot of that will get covered, but I think unilaterally forcing down some kind of decision is going to lead to problems.' If 'heads have to be hammered together,' to ensure synergy, 'and the political leadership has to get involved, so be it.'

Before the announcement about creating theatre commands, were the chiefs consulted? Air Chief Marshal Major (Retd) asked Lieutenant General Dua (Retd). The theatre command issues came up only after Bipin Rawat took over as CDS in January 2020, replied Lieutenant General Dua (Retd). He had hung up his boots two years earlier. The only discussions on theatre commands at that point were all very academic. When Air Chief Marshal N.A.K. Browne (Retd), asked a similar question, there wasn't much clarity either. 'I have no idea at all. I retired 15-16 years ago. I only read newspapers,' said Admiral Prakash (Retd). 'None of us would have any idea,' agreed Air Chief Marshal Major (Retd). 'It has been more than 10-11 years (since I retired).' Also unsure, Lieutenant General Dua (Retd) replied 'the chiefs *would* have been consulted, there *would* have been differences... the debate that came out in the media was sort of untimely, unseemly.' He felt that the decisions haven't been made, the discussions are still going on and if statements have been made, in reply to questions during a seminar, 'that particular contentious statement of (the IAF) being a supporting arm (made by General Rawat)... (was) not a policy statement'.

It isn't about the statement, interjected Admiral Prakash (Retd), it's the fact that the issue was discussed in public. The remark (by General Rawat) was made, then the air chief (then Air Chief Marshal R.K.S. Bhadauria) felt obliged to say something much milder, but the very fact that it was discussed in public, an issue of such sensitive nature, indicates to the public at large that it has not been discussed in the teak panelled, elegant Chiefs of Staff Committee room, which is the right place for such issues.'

Yes, acknowledged Lieutenant General Dua (Retd), it did create a flutter, but he felt that 'even if it creates a little national debate, there is no big deal because we will still sit down and... decide this behind closed doors. And then, we will know.'

QUESTIONS AND ANSWERS

During the question-and-answer session that followed, Mr Amit Kowshish, a senior official in the Defence Ministry, now retired, asked: is the integration of civil and military components moving in the right direction, considering that the Joint Secretaries posted in the DMA are managing establishment, coordination, works and parliamentary affairs? None of these areas, he suggested, were cutting edge. Second, he asked what the CDS would be able to do if the (responsibility) of the defence of India was handed over to the DMA? As General Dua clarified: 'What is it that CDS will be able to do that he cannot do right now, if he's given the responsibility for the defence of India?'

In reply, Admiral Prakash (Retd) noted that while he didn't know about the portfolios of civilian officers in the DMA, 'every civil servant who comes to the Defence Ministry is a transient person. He's hoping for and looking forward to something that is better than the Defence Ministry.' This is because there's no cadre that's 'devoted to national security,' he argued. 'With utmost respect for many able civil servants, there is no sense of belonging to the Defence Ministry, which it would be if he was actually trained and devoted to this cadre. So many of them come and go, perhaps they come back for a second time.' And the financial advisors are not advisors, 'they don't advise you how to spend money, how to spend the budget, they wait for you to make your first mistake, then they pounce on you and there's an audit objection and a parliamentary question and so on.' If there's no integration in the Defence Ministry, it is because the civilians are 'looking out for their careers. We were told by Mr Naresh Chandra (former Cabinet Secretary) that if we create a National Security Cadre in the IAS or Civil Services, it will be harmful to their career prospects.'

Answering Mr Kowshish's question about the responsibility for the defence of India, he said it was 'common sense' that if a CDS has been appointed, he would have the responsibility and not a civil servant. 'He will find ways and means of doing things. Right now, the Defence Secretary is more concerned about acquisition. He's the Chief Financial Officer of the Defence Ministry. He has to go to parliament and answer questions. He is not interested in the defence of India and every part thereof. It is not fair to give him this, nor is it correct.'

Replying to a question by Major General J.P. Alex (Retd) about the service chiefs being responsible for training, equipping and administration and the present commands, suitably restructured into theatre commands reporting to the CDS, looking at the 'threat dimensions', Lieutenant General Hooda (Retd) said that is currently what is being worked on. So far, a lot of the command-and-control issues, the responsibility of the chiefs and the CDS and the restructuring of the DMA are yet to be decided.

Group Captain Johnson Chacko and Mr Ravindra Pal Singh had similar questions about integration, the creation of theatre commands with permanently allocated weaponry and how the Air Force would handle it. In his reply, Air Chief Marshal Major (Retd) pointed out that the United States had a thousand aircraft in the Pacific Command and as many in the Central Command. 'If we had those kinds of resources, most certainly you could allocate them permanently. But given our resources, we have to make use of them most economically.' Giving the theatre commands the aircraft they need, rather than keeping it in places where they are located, keeping in mind the threats, would be much more inconvenient and if aircraft are being bought for separate missions (like air defence or ground attack), it would be very expensive.'

Air Force assets (primarily, the fighter squadrons) are divided in five operational commands, Lieutenant General Dua (Retd) added. 'Whatever number of integrated commands is raised, eventually, whether two or three or four, the air assets would then be divided amongst these integrated structures.' If there's a requirement even now, air assets 'are allocated from one theatre or rebalanced from one theatre to another depending on the requirement. And so will the case be whenever these integrated structures are raised. As the air force is more "mobile" and therefore flexible, they can move very quickly from one theatre to another.'

India is creating theatre commands in the way other countries have done, asked Brigadier Pankaj Sinha, but considering the terrain and the threats, primarily land-based, will theatre commands actually work?

India's restructuring is unique, India's not replicating what any other country has done, replied Admiral Prakash (Retd). There should be clarity about what Iindia needs to achieve by creating theatre commands, 'the topmost objectives should be 'jointness, economy, giving more power to the actual war-fighters in the field, and separating staff and warfighting functions from New Delhi, where the chiefs are currently performing both.' If the goals are clear, the formations that will come up keeping them in mind, will be appropriate for India's terrain and different kinds of threats, he added.

Agreeing with Admiral Prakash (Retd) about the need to integrate—altogether 66 countries have already gone ahead with it—Lieutenant General Dua (Retd) acknowledged that the three chiefs were 'saddled with too much responsibility. They are operational commanders… they are also responsible for capability building. He was confident about a new integrated structure, one that would be successful, would be much better.' The theatre commands do not have to be ready in three years, he clarified, replying to a question by Mr Harish Shah—the government has asked for jointness in three years, the words 'theatre commands' have not been used at all. Once the services agree to the new structures, government approval will be required, but it won't be necessary for the PMO to coordinate or oversee the effort,' he said.

Also hopeful, Lieutenant General Hooda (Retd) regretted that 'our current structures are not suited for joint fighting and whatever modules we are going to create… will be well thought out'. And this 'will be a much better model' than the one currently existing with the Army, Navy and Air Force having commands away from each other.

Asked about the future of the Strategic Forces Command, commonly known as India's nuclear command, Admiral Prakash (Retd) pointed out it was created in 2001 after the Group of Ministers (GoM) report in the wake of the Kargil war. 'It's well settled and it's doing quite well. The SFC is not involved in any of this reform and reorganization.'

As for the 'theaterization business, whatever it means,' as he unhappily called it, Admiral Prakash felt 'we could have focused on jointness; there is much more that could have been done in the last year and a half…. We could have altered the syllabi of our staff college and our other institutions, we could have churned out a whole set of joint staff officers who would have manned the billets of the theatre commands,' first as component commanders and then, as theatre commanders. 'This is something that needs to be attended (to) urgently, the need to change the designation of the Staff College from Defence Services to Joint Staff College, have a common syllabus which will produce staff officers who can man billets in integrated commands.'

One way of negotiating through the current difficulties relating to the creation of the theatre commands is to go back to 2001, and see how the tri-service Andaman and Nicobar Command came up, he said. 'It's worth our while to go back 20 years and see what happened in Port Blair, how things were resolved. How does the Andaman and Nicobar Command function today? What do the component commanders do? What functions do the staff perform? There may be some lessons' there for those working on creating the theatre commands.

Yes, changing the syllabi at the Staff College and other institutions would have helped, agreed Lieutenant General Dua (Retd), but beyond training majors and officers of equivalent rank in the Navy and Air Force, 'exposure' and 'serving in each other's headquarters and units' is 'going to make a difference'. Even the Goldwater-Nichols Act (in the United States) there are incentives for officers to participate in 'joint' course along with officers of other services. There are more incentives for a stint (in another service.) 'In fact, I have suggested that you make it mandatory for a two-star officer to have done one tenure. You make it mandatory for a three-star officer to have done a couple of tenures in joint organizations or establishments. I think that would make a lot of difference'. I have served in the Andamans and I realize how easy it is for me to understand that when the Navy says 'very good', that's something that they always have to say. When, say, there's a fire in the engine room, the captain first says 'very good!' Well, that's on the lighter side.

Summing up, Lieutenant General Dua (Retd) said there's consensus on integration, 'because we cannot go it alone in these present times when warfare is actually acquiring a very complex dynamic.' It is good, he said that the planning process has begun, that there's 'churning taking place,' with the armed forces, their chiefs and their staff taking decisions. There's also consensus about better civil-military relations and the requirement of an apex-level 'guidance document because we need to get the leadership really involved, hands on, in matters concerning the security of the state.'

There were contentious issues during the debate, he admitted—air power being the most significant. There are discussions on the subject among retired people, in academia and in the media. It's a healthy sign, but like Admiral Prakash (Retd), he agreed it would need to also happen privately, in South Block's teak-panelled rooms. Meaningful conversations, he felt, were a must as they'd lead to consensus, and eventually, an integrated and certainly formidable armed forces.

Lieutenant General Dua (Retd) hoped, and on behalf of the other participants as well, that after discussions India will have a better war-fighting model and, hopefully, within a certain timeline. The new systems are really essential, and if more time is required to arrive at a consensus within the armed forces, that leeway must be granted. And that is where the discussions ended. It's now up to the armed forces and the government to consider the available philosophies and arrive at the decisions about integration, the consultation with the political leadership, the creation of theatre commands and what the role of the Air Force is to be.

X

Towards Progressive Defence Reforms

Bipin Rawat

I would like to first give a very brief overview of the geopolitical landscape around the world. The disintegration of the Soviet Union led to a unipolar world. At the time, geopolitical thinkers like Francis Fukuyama and Samuel Huntington professed their theses and people started believing that a unipolar world was ahead and that the US will reign over the world for years to come. This, they felt, would be a good mechanism, a kind of capitalistic parliamentary democracy. This did happen, and several capitalistic democracies began to take shape till about 2000.

Things began to change after the millennium, and we started reverting to old systems. Once again there was concern whether Samuel Huntington's theory would prove right when he said there will be a clash of civilizations. He mentioned eight civilizations and how they would clash. He also said that the Confucius or the Sinic civilization could actually join hands with the Islamic civilization to counter Western civilization. Whether or not this will happen, only time will tell, but we are seeing some kind of jointmenship. I use this term also to refer to the link between the Sinic and

the Islamic civilizations. China is now making friends with
Iran and moving towards Turkey. They have stepped into
Afghanistan, and they will continue to do so sooner rather
than later. Therefore, there will be a clash of civilizations
with Western civilization. And let's not forget Yoval Noah
Hariri's version of what is going to happen in the twenty-first
century. So, this is a world in turmoil.

At one stage the thinking was that perhaps a unipolar
world might be good because at least a democratic country
like America could ensure more democracies, leading to
peace and happiness. In reality, more wars were being fought
at that time in the unipolar world.

Then came the rise of China, much faster than people
envisaged. Therefore, I believe we are again heading back
to a bipolar or a multipolar world. Is that good or bad for
the international community? Only time will tell. But I think
what we are certainly seeing is more aggression on the part
of nations, especially the one that is trying to make inroads
into a bipolar world or making its presence felt—China—and
becoming more and more aggressive. And we share land
borders with them. Therefore, it is time for us to start looking
at our strategies in terms of how we will deal with the two
borders which are aggressive neighbours and adversaries—
Pakistan on the western front and China on the northern.

We also need to consider transformation for betterment
and ensure that the national security architecture that we
want to evolve is capable of dealing with the kinds of threats
we are seeing at our borders, as also the internal security
threats that are emerging. Who is going to do all this?

For this, some kind of jointmenship or integration amongst
all the security forces is essential. When a war is thrust upon
us, there are security dimensions that are not just related to

the security of borders—they are all encompassing, including food and health security. Therefore, one has to ensure that the economy is protected. When nations do go to war, it is not just the militaries that go to war, the nation also goes to war. If we work on this premise then all organizations of our nation must work together, at least those which are responsible for the security of the nation. Therefore, there is an increasing need to ensure not just integration within the services, within the paramilitary forces and the Central Armed Police Forces (CAPF), but also within the civilian organization—we have to integrate them all.

At higher defence levels, the Chief of the Defence Staff (CDS) has been created but, to date, is concentrating on integration between the security agencies and the security forces. But gradually, with the creation of the the the Department of Military Affairs (DMA) and along with other ministries, a governmental approach is being adopted to look into these security issues.

Many thoughts that Mr Vohra elucidated in his introduction are actually beginning to take shape in the government. I do not know whether this was a sixth sense prevailing within the political leadership, but things have actually come into the pipeline and we will see these taking shape in the future.

Coming to the kind of wars that will be fought in the future: their character and nature are changing very fast; wars may not necessarily be fought the way they were in the past, which were battles of attrition, man on man, gun on gun, aircraft on aircraft.

Countries and nations will employ technology to their advantage to put pressure on their adversaries. Therefore, when we talk of national power today we believe it comprises the pillars of diplomacy, information, military and economy.

I think it is time to look at technology as the fifth pillar of national power. Technology can no longer be considered a progressive national power by the international community.

Why are we looking at this kind of jointness and integration?

Today, the Army, Navy and Air Force, the Coast Guard, Ministry of Defence (MoD) and the CAPF provide support to the military during combat and even during peace time, and the Border Security Force (BSF) in J&K operates shoulder to shoulder and shares similar responsibilities as the military. The need of the hour is to integrate the efforts of the three services and any others that support the war effort.

There is a western adversary which will continue to create proxy wars in our country and keep expanding the zone of proxy. It is happening in J&K. They are attempting to do the same in Punjab once again, and trying to spread into other parts of our country as well. A weaker adversary like Pakistan will always keep us engaged through proxy war. And they are in fact a proxy of our northern adversary—China. That is the next issue we have to look at. But as far as the northern adversary is concerned, since we have unsettled borders with them, and they have shown aggression on the east coast on the South China Sea and with nations in that area, are they likely to show aggression on our northern borders?

Whether that happens in the form of direct aggression, or through technology, we have to be prepared. And this preparation can only happen if we work together.

There is now scope for space-based systems and how we can engage through space jointly. We have to start looking at our cyber capabilities, at the AI engines, and how these can support the military. Technology is becoming the need of the hour and we must ensure that all the three defence services understand the importance of it.

Why are we looking at reorganization? When the CDS was created, the appointment was Chief of Defence Staff. He was expected to ensure that the three services work in unison and through jointness. And in doing so we realized that if we have to work against our western adversary or against our northern adversary, we have to work jointly. For this reason we thought of creating theatre commands—one theatre which looks after our western adversary and another theatre that looks after our northern adversary.

What is wrong with the present system? Here, I would like to draw on an analogy from 1971. In 1971, the armed forces, the Army, Navy and Air Force, worked under the central leadership of General Sam Manekshaw because a charismatic leader was needed to take control of the situation. He was the Chief of the Army Staff, but was becoming the principal advisor to the government at that time, with Admiral Nanda and Air Chief Marshall Lal supporting him. I prefer not to use the term support which seems to have become unsavoury, but the fact is that they were all working together in an integrated and joint manner.

But on the eastern front, an eastern theatre was created headed by General Jagjit Singh Aurora, along with his naval and air force counterparts, working in unison with him very closely. Vice Admiral Dewan, who was the Eastern Naval Commander, was working with him and Air Marshal Krishnan from the Eastern Air Command. They had built a joint team which fought the war in the eastern theatre and achieved tremendous success because of it. But how were they able to achieve jointness? This is because we were preparing for the war from April and it finally took place in

December. They had all this time to work together, work out their plans together, and thus bring in jointness.

Were they allocated resources at the beginning of the war? Yes, they were. The Army had its resources. The Air Force gave some dedicated resources to the eastern theatre, and so did the Navy. The Eastern Naval Command was tasked to be prepared for the Western Front on the Arabian Sea, but the primary charter at that time was the Bay of Bengal and they supported the effort against East Pakistan, now Bangladesh.

The Western Front was under the command of General Candeth operating from Simla, and there was also a Southern Army Command under General Bewoor operating from Poona. Admiral Kohli was looking after the Western Naval Command and an Air Force Component Commander. They were working together. But the problem here was that there were two Army Component Commanders, a Naval Commander and an Air Force Commander. Were they integrated in the same manner as in the east? That question remains to be answered.

The Western Army Commander felt that he could get a decisive victory. The Southern Army Commander thought he could get a decisive victory. The air resources were being split between the two according to who should get better support. The Navy also had resources, so they did not want to be left out. They had acquired some patrol boats from Russia at that time. They suggested using them innovatively in a way that even the Russians would not have envisaged. Finally, the patrol boats were directed to attack Karachi harbour, and this is how the Navy went into battle.

We saw success all right, but I do not think the battle was integrated. Each one was planning on its own. The battle was quite integrated on the eastern theatre because of the time and the planning that went into it. What happened on the eastern front? By about 7 or 8 December, the Pakistani Air Force had been completely decimated by our Air Force because we could do a Tangail landing, which hastened the capture of Dhaka, and the troops were able to move in faster because one can land behind enemy lines through an airborne operation. So an air–land battle was being played out—a joint Air Force and Army operating together, and then a blockade from the sea by the Navy—no one could escape from East Pakistan. That is how we got 93,000 prisoners, which included about 11,000 civilians. This is what jointness can do.

By about 8 or 9 December, because the battle was being fought in Longewala and the Pakistanis were getting the better of us in the Chamb sector, the Air Force was diverted to the Western Front. So the allocation and reallocation of resources took place even in 1971 and led to success.

How did this happen? Because we were operating in a joint manner and had worked out a mechanism of integration. We have studied the 1971 war and we are trying to understand if it can work now. Looking towards Pakistan, we have four Army Commands: the Northern Command, Udhampur; the Western Command, Chandigarh; the Southwestern Command, Jaipur; and Southern Command, Pune.

Three Air Force Commands look after that front. There is a Western Air Command in Delhi, a Southwestern Air Command in Gandhinagar, and a Southern Air Command in Trivandrum. These are all responsible for the Western Front and in the event of a war there is also a Western Naval Command at Mumbai and a Southern Naval Command, but this is more responsible as a training command of the Navy. On the east is the Central Air Command of the Air Force in Allahabad which can focus on both fronts. It can look at the east and the west. There is an Eastern Air Command at Shillong; the Army has a Central Command looking at the northern borders; an Eastern Command looking at the Northern borders; and again, a split Northern Command looking both at the north and west.

Therefore, there are 17 Commands responsible for coordinating operations against both our adversaries. Who will be our primary adversary, who will be our secondary adversary is something that the government will decide and the armed forces under the CDS will recommend to the government the best way of combating these adversaries and also addressing our internal security situation.

We are now looking at creating theatre commands, one on the west with Pakistan. They will have one leader, from the Army, Navy or Air Force, whoever is best suited for the job. He will have his Air Force Component Commander who will become his advisor for Air Defence and offensive operations, and the Naval Component Commander will advise him on naval operations. We will be prepared to fight the operation on the Western Front the way we fought the operation in Bangladesh, while at the same time ensuring internal security which has to be integrated at the time of war.

There is also some thought about generating more forces for the Army and others by allocating some of the Army's tasks to the CAPF. They are as good as us, they train with us, they have weapon systems which are equally as good as ours; we are now looking at integrated purchase of systems as well. Therefore, they can also take on some defensive tasks while the Army's on-ground holding role is released for offensive tasks.

We are also looking at our northern neighbour and talking about creating a command. China has created one command for the entire Tibet Autonomous Region and Xinjiang, called the Western Theatre Commander. He is responsible for all the ground and Air Forces operating in that area. This is how they conduct operations. We too are looking to create one force with the Navy, the Eastern Naval Command and the Air Force Component Commanders operating with them.

Whoever heads this command, whether it is the Army, Navy or Air Force, the other two services will play an advisory role so that they also integrate with them and we fight a battle which is joint.

Apart from our land borders, we also have the Indian Ocean to defend. This is becoming increasingly important because of increasing trade and the way the navies from various countries operate in this region.

Therefore, as we have said, why don't we have one command called the National Maritime Command looking at the Indian Ocean region, or the Indo-Pacific as we now call it? There is a Western Naval Command and an Eastern Naval Command which we want integrated as one theatre under a theatre commander who is responsible for the entire Indian Ocean region as one entity. Then there are island territories which are excellent islands of resistance in the Indian Ocean region.

We have created the CINCAN, the Commander Andaman and Nicobar Islands. He is the first integrated commander after the Kargil war and after the Kargil War Committee of 2003. Along with that, we created the Integrated Defence Staff (IDS) headquarters in Delhi. As of now, the CINCAN, who is looking after the island territories, does not function under the Chief of the Naval Staff or the Navy. He reports directly to headquarters IDS or to the present CDS. Therefore, while we have an Indian Ocean region, the land territory there actually belongs to the seas and must be controlled by one Component Commander, who is the Naval Commander, and resources must be made available to him because these are islands of resistance—look at the Mounts of Malacca and all the Lombok states—we can defend our territory better if we are well-equipped and prepared to operate in an integrated manner in the entire Indian Ocean region. That is why we need to have a maritime command.

The use of airspace is becoming more and more complex. It is no longer the aircraft, the fighter, the transport helicopters that are going to be using the airspace, so there is a need to coordinate all the activities amongst the users of the airspace. Today we have missiles, rocket and artillery systems which are firing at long range. Today, when an artillery round lands 48 km across, it goes at a height of 15,000 feet or 15 km. This is where the Air Force is also operating, and along with nap-of-the earth flying, there are missiles and rockets firing in the air as well. Today commanding officers have tactical Unmanned Aerial Vehicles (UAVs)—who is going to coordinate all this? We don't want fratricide in the airspace! Therefore, to prevent this, we must have an Air Component Commander who will look after air defence of the airspace above the land. For this reason we said we need to look at air defence as one theatre and commanded by one person who will control it. Either the air headquarters takes the responsibility or the Air Chief who already has multifarious other tasks: offensive tasks, tasks in support of ground operations, tasks in support of the sea, and also air defence. We therefore suggested a dedicated Air Defence Commander responsible for the airspace above, operating under the Chief of Staff and then under the Chiefs of Staff Committee to see how to exercise command control. For example, today, we are told that the Air Force could be operating anywhere because they can operate at long ranges and have speed. So, you could have an aircraft operating from Allahabad or even from Tezpur and coming to the western theatre. But what route will it take? It will fly possibly in the hinterland, but rockets and missiles could also be firing there. Can you have missiles and rockets firing simultaneously when the aircraft is coming east to west and rockets firing south to north? You could well be crashing into each other. Somebody had to take control and decide who has priority, whether the aircraft should be allowed to operate at that time or whether the guns should fire or fall silent.

This system is followed in air defence too. Air defence is the responsibility of the Air Force. Even the Army Air Defence sources are controlled by the Air Force because air defence is the Charter of the Air Force. But today, because the Army Air Defence knows that they have to take orders from the Air Force, they do so. Air Defence knows if the guns can fire or have to be held tight. But the artillery does not. The Army does not take orders from the Air Force, and its artillery, missiles or UAVs are being launched by the Commanding Officers who know little about this.

Someone has to give every user of the airspace command and control; those best suited for this are the people who understand the airspace above them and that would be the Air Force. This is why we said we need to have an Air Defence Command to control any user in the airspace.

How do we split resources? We have recently imported 36 Rafael which are two squadrons. One squadron has been housed at Ambala and the second squadron at Halwara. If the resources are so few, should we be splitting them? But the need of the hour is to have developed the capacity by splitting these resources *ab initio*. One is with Western Air Command and one with Eastern Air Command, but when the time comes, one can ensure that both of them operate either on the Western Front or the Northern Front. So, before the war starts, resources are allocated and depending on how the threat evolves, resources can be allocated accordingly.

Therefore, the mindset that air, army or other resources cannot be reallocated is not entirely correct. Grouping and regrouping of forces before combat, during combat, and after combat will always take place.

The next issue to highlight, as already mentioned, is that the armed forces have to be prepared to fight with a technological orientation. If we think that there will be a battle of attrition and our neighbour or our adversary will come head on with tanks and infantry, frontal and suicidal attacks, it may not happen. In fact, we may find that the troops in the depths may get affected first and one will not know when the war started because the adversary may launch a cyber attack. The first affected might be our railway systems, banking and financial establishments without our knowing that the adversary is at war with us. Gradually, our military systems will also be affected by cyber attacks.

Today, space technology can be used for ensuring continuous surveillance. There are missiles and rockets which can be guided to destroy at any time. Therefore, as mentioned, the depth objectives which are where the logistic echelons are and where reserves are parked may actually be in battle first, and those at the frontline may actually be very safe at first. This the adversary will treat as psychological warfare by using social resources, information warfare, and try and prevent us from going into battle in the manner in which we had planned. It will instead make you fight the battle in the way it has been planned. This is what we need to understand and be prepared for.

I would like to comment on a point Mr Vohra mentioned: military history. The policy plan is to declassify all histories after 25 years of a particular incident, unless there are specific reasons not to declassify a particular part of the history. The Department of Personnel and Training is looking at this as a new specialization. If somebody wants to join the MoD, he/she can take credits, undergo courses on defence and security issues, and then get posted to the MoD. This new venture is at the Prime Minister's direction.

Editor and Contributors

N.N. VOHRA, Life Trustee and former President of the India International Centre, Delhi (2017–22), is a recipient of the Padma Vibhushan (2007). While serving in the IAS (1959–94) he held various important positions, including Secretary Defence Production, Defence Secretary, Home and Justice Secretary and, after retirement, as Principal Secretary to the Prime Minister. Served as Governor of the erstwhile State of J&K during 2008–2018; has long years of experience in the security administration arena. After the Indo-China conflict, he joined the Special Services Bureau (in the Intelligence Bureau), received training from the SAS of UK, and operated in the West Himalayan region. Served as Home Secretary Panjab in the turbulent period after Operation Blue Star (1984). Author of *Safeguarding India* (2016); has edited 15 books on varied themes.

C. UDAY BHASKAR, Director, Society for Policy Studies, New Delhi, retired from the Indian Navy in early 2007 after 37 years of service, and has the rare distinction of having headed three think tanks. He was previously Director, National Maritime Foundation (2009–11) and earlier with the Institute for Defence Studies and Analyses, New Delhi from 1989 where he served as a Senior Fellow, Deputy Director (1996–2004) and later as Offg. Director of the Institute till late 2005. Subsequently he was appointed Member-Secretary of the Government of India Task Force on 'Global Strategic Developments', a report submitted to the Prime Minister of India.

PHILIP CAMPOSE, 35th Vice Chief of the Indian Army, retired after about 41 years of military service, on 31 July 2015. An alumnus of St Xavier's School, Delhi, and the National Defence Academy, Pune, he served his early years in a Battalion of the 9th Gorkha Rifles, before being transferred into the Mechanised Infantry Regiment. During his service, he developed expertise in mechanized warfare, counter insurgency, United Nations peacekeeping, nuclear warfare, counter terrorism and strategic planning. As Lieutenant General, he also held the important posts of Director General Perspective Planning at Army Headquarters and Army Commander of the Western Command.

SUJAN R. CHINOY is the Director General of the Manohar Parrikar Institute for Defence Studies and Analyses, New Delhi. A career diplomat from 1981 to 2018, he held several important diplomatic assignments, including as Ambassador to Japan. A specialist on East Asia, China and Politico-Security issues, he anchored negotiations with China on the boundary dispute in the Ministry of External Affairs. On deputation to the National Security Council Secretariat, his expertise covered defence and security issues, particularly in South Asia and the extended neighbourhood of the Indo-Pacific. He is also the Indian Chair of the Think-20 Core Group during India's G20 Presidency.

SRINJOY CHOWDHURY is Consulting Editor (National Affairs), Times Now. He joined *Sunday Magazine* in 1984, and then worked for *The Telegraph* and *The Statesman*. After his first book, *Despatches from Kargil*, he co-authored *Flight into Fear* on the hijacking of IC–814 to Kandahar. 'Tahrir', about the Arab Spring, is part of The Dilemma of Popular Sovereignty in the Middle East. Chowdhury's report, 'The View from an Indian Television Newsroom: What Makes us Different', is included in Media at Work in China and India.

DEEPENDRA S. HOODA served in the Indian Army for forty years. He retired as the Army Commander of Northern Command where he was responsible for operations along the Line of Control with Pakistan and the Line of Actual Control with China in Ladakh. He also commanded the counterinsurgency operations in Kashmir. Hooda is a co-founder of the Council for Strategic and Defense Research, a New Delhi based think-tank, and a Senior Fellow at the Delhi Policy Group.

ARUN PRAKASH was India's 18th Naval Chief and served as Chairman's Chief of Staff, retiring in end-2006. A naval-aviator by specialization, he has held appointments in command of ships, air squadrons and a naval air station. In flag-rank he commanded the Eastern Fleet, the National Defence Academy, the Andaman & Nicobar Joint Command and the Western Naval Command. During the 1971 war he saw action with the Indian Air Force and was awarded the Vir Chakra for gallantry. Post-retirement, he served two terms as member of the National Security Advisory Board, and was Chairman of the National Maritime Foundation. Currently, he holds a Distinguished Chair at India's Naval War College. He writes and speaks on strategic and maritime affairs.

BIPIN RAWAT PVSM UYSM AVSM YSM SM VSM ADC (16 March 1958–8 December 2021), Padma Vibhushan, won the Sword of Honour at the Indian Military Academy and rose to become the Chief of Army Staff. As the senior-most Chief of Staff amongst the three Services, he served as the Chairman of the Chiefs of Staff Committee of the Indian Armed Forces (September to December 2019). He was appointed the first Chief of Defence Staff (CDS) of the Indian Armed Forces in January 2020 and served until his untimely death in a helicopter crash in December 2021.

AJAY SAHNI is the Executive Director of the Institute for Conflict Management, the South Asia Terrorism Portal and Khalistan Extremism Monitor; Publisher and Editor, *South Asia Intelligence Review, Faultlines: K.P.S. Gill Journal of Conflict and Resolution*. He served as a Member of the (Madhukar Gupta) Committee on the Restructuring of the Ministry of Home Affairs and of the Police Modernisation and Strengthening Committee, Uttar Pradesh. He is a Distinguished Fellow of the United Services Institute. He has researched and written extensively on issues relating to conflict, politics and development in South Asia, and has participated in advisory projects undertaken for various national or state governments.

ARJUN SUBRAMANIAM, AVSM (Retd) is a retired fighter pilot from the IAF, a military historian and the author of *India's Wars: A Military History: 1947–1971* sequel titled *Full Spectrum: India's Wars 1972–2020*. He is currently the President's Chair of Excellence in National Security at the National Defence College and an Adjunct Faculty member at the Naval War College.

After retirement from the Indian Air Force in 2017, he has been a Visiting Fellow at Harvard and Oxford universities and a Visiting Professor at the Fletcher School of Law and Diplomacy, Ashoka University, and the Kautilya School of Public Policy.

Milton Keynes UK
Ingram Content Group UK Ltd.
UKHW030411030224
437193UK00011B/261/J